GEORGE Kelly

Key Figures in Counselling and Psychotherapy

Series editor: Windy Dryden

The *Key Figures in Counselling and Psychotherapy* series of books provides a concise, accessible introduction to the lives, contributions and influence of the leading innovators whose theoretical and practical work has had a profound impact on counselling and psychotherapy. The series includes comprehensive overviews of:

Sigmund Freud
by Michael Jacobs

Eric Berne
by Ian Stewart

Carl Rogers
by Brian Thorne

Melanie Klein
by Julia Segal

Fritz Perls
by Petrūska Clarkson and Jennifer Mackewn

Aaron T. Beck
by Marjorie E. Weishaar

Albert Ellis
by Joseph Yankura and Windy Dryden

Joseph Wolpe
by Roger Poppen

George Kelly
by Fay Fransella

D. W. Winnicott
by Michael Jacobs

GEORGE Kelly

Fay Fransella

SAGE Publications
London • Thousand Oaks • New Delhi

First published 1995

SAGE Publications Ltd
6 Bonhill Street
London EC2A 4PU

SAGE Publications Inc
2455 Teller Road
Thousand Oaks, California 91320

SAGE Publications India Pvt Ltd
32, M-Block Market
Greater Kailash – I
New Delhi 110 048

British Library Cataloguing in Publication data

A catalogue record for this book is available from the British Library

ISBN 0 8039 8494 4
ISBN 0 8039 8495 2 (pbk)

Library of Congress catalog card number 95-071357

Typeset by Mayhew Typesetting, Rhayader, Powys
Printed in Great Britain by Biddles Ltd, Guildford, Surrey

Contents

Preface

Without the patience of the series editor, Professor Windy Dryden and the counselling editor of Sage Publications, this book would not have been finished. It was not so much that looking at George Kelly's contributions to psychotherapy turned out to be so difficult: it was the man himself. I started on the middle chapters – the middle always seems a good place to start – and all was going well. It was when I came to draft the first chapter that the trouble started. I had used, with the permission of his widow, Gladys Kelly, large parts of his own autobiographical sketch to base my views on. Windy wrote back that it was a half-hearted OK, but 'where is the man?'

That was quite a shock. I suddenly realized that George Kelly the person was not in the chapter because virtually nothing has been written about him. He was a private man and so had written little about himself. My personal acquaintanceship with him had been all too limited. After a period of near panic, I decided the only thing to do was to write to a sample of his ex-students and ask for any impressions, stories and opinions they cared to give me. I also decided to search his unpublished as well as his published writings to see if they said anything about 'the man'.

My list ended up with eighteen people on it. Not everyone replied and some did not feel they knew Kelly well enough to contribute. But several people gave me invaluable help. First and foremost, I must thank Rue Cromwell, who became involved in my search and without whose help the chapter could not have been written. Then there were Brendan Maher, Al Landfield, William Perry, Franz Epting, and Esther Cava who all gave me many examples of their interactions with and opinions of George Kelly.

From these, coupled with some vital insights gleaned from his own writings, I managed to piece together some indication of the sort of person George Kelly might have been. The problem became one of knowing when to stop. Each new piece of information opened up other avenues. What I am now convinced of is that George Kelly, the man, is embedded – much more than I first thought – in his own writings. But stop I had to. I make no claim whatever that I have got anywhere near the 'truth' – but that is as it should be. George Kelly was a highly original thinker whose influence still continues today. He was also a man committed to establishing the profession of clinical psychology, of which psychotherapy was a part. I would thank Brendan Maher especially here for giving me important background information.

There are some other people who have given me invaluable help with various theoretical points. In particular I turned to Bill Warren for help with the philosophical aspects of Kelly's work. I have no training in philosophy and so feel very diffident about delving into this field. Bill showed great patience as we wandered through the philosophical undergrowth. Responsibility for what appears in this book is, of course, entirely mine. Ray Evans and Chris Thorman gave me great help over specific aspects of Kelly's work. Phil Salmon sent me off on what turned out to be a most important search – 'What sort of teacher did Kelly think he was?' This was nicely linked with William Perry's question, 'Who did Kelly think he was?'

I am most grateful to Gladys Kelly who, some years ago now, allowed me to browse through Kelly's unpublished boxes of papers and to take whatever photocopies I liked. She also gave permission for me to use them as I saw fit. As the reader will soon find out, I have made considerable use of them.

The Style of the Work

The first thing that will be obvious to any reader is the wealth of quotations throughout the text. This is partly because George Kelly was a brilliant writer and can put over a point far better than I can. But it is equally to do with my attempt to give as much of a feel for 'the man' as possible. Apart from the quotations from many authors, there are also, of course, the accounts given by all the ex-students. To avoid having too many citations of 'personal communication', I have deliberately left those out when giving such accounts.

George Kelly's ideas may be more difficult to summarize than those of some other psychotherapists because he did not write as a psychotherapist. He wrote as a psychologist describing a theory and a philosophical system that applies to every one of us in our daily lives. Psychotherapy is just one application of his theory and philosophy. My criterion for selection of topics to be covered in depth or superficially is one of usefulness and potential interest to psychotherapists and counsellors.

Above all, this is not intended to be a definitive account of George Kelly and his work. Examples of research and ideas are presented in an unashamedly uncritical way. It seemed to me that it was more important to talk about Kelly's thinking, and what people have done with that, than to look to see whether any particular line of thought has been shown to be valid. Kelly's philosophy of constructive alternativism when applied to scientific endeavour encourages one to ask questions in order to raise other questions, in the full knowledge that one's last question will soon be overlaid when new evidence comes to light.

There is the usual problem over gender language and whether to use the first or third person. I have opted for a variety of ways of avoiding being sexist and have mixed the first and third person as appropriate.

Lastly, George Kelly's two-volume work, *The Psychology of Personal Constructs* (1955a) was reprinted by Routledge in 1991, in collaboration with the Centre for Personal Construct Psychology, London. Page references are therefore to the 1991 edition.

Layout of the Book

This book has the same structure as all other books in the series. In this case, the first and second chapters are twice as long as the others. The first chapter is about George Kelly's life, his personality and how these relate to his work. Its length perhaps reflects the struggle it has been to get this far; it demonstrates the principle that the more is written about a subject the less is known about it. The second chapter is about his major theoretical contributions to psychotherapy. His contributions are many, both from a theoretical and a practical perspective. So the chapter is in two parts. The first part discusses Kelly's contributions to the theory of psychotherapy generally and the second part focuses on his theoretical contributions to the practice of psychotherapy.

Next comes a chapter on Kelly's practical contributions to psychotherapy. This mentions his major assessment tool, the repertory grid. But no more has been said about this than is required to give the reader an overview of what 'a grid' is about. In some senses, the grid has tended to overshadow Kelly's theory and philosophy. But it is only a tool to be used by a psychotherapist as and when it seems useful – *an essential part of personal construct psychotherapy it is not.*

Chapter 4 is concerned with criticisms of the theory and their rebuttals. Of interest here is the fact that some criticisms are levelled by personal construct psychologists against their fellow personal construct psychologists. I think that shows the theory and philosophy are alive and kicking.

The last chapter is an overview of Kelly's contribution to psychotherapy and any later developments. One major difficulty here was to choose which developments stemming from Kelly's work to include. My additional criterion was to choose topics that have been followed up over the years. It turns out that there is a heavy weighting of British examples. I think this has happened because work started in the UK well before anywhere else – the British have been at it longer than most.

Acknowledgements

The author and the publishers would like to thank the following for permission to reproduce the following material.

We thank Gladys Kelly for allowing much unpublished material of the late George Kelly to be included in this volume, particularly for the extensive use made of his personal account of the details of his education and professional life. All this text and figures 1 and 2 copyright © George Kelly's estate.

The Centre for Personal Construct Psychology, London, for excerpts printed from 'A brief introduction to personal construct theory', 'Behaviour is an experiment', 'Values, knowledge and social control', and *The Function of Interpretation in Psychotherapy: 1. Interpretation as a way of life.*

George Kelly's two-volume *The Psychology of Personal Constructs* was published by Routledge in 1991 in association with the Centre for Personal Construct Psychology, London. We thank Routledge for giving permission to quote extensively from these volumes in view of this association.

John Wiley & Sons for excerpts from Bob Neimeyer, Chapter 5 in *Personal Construct Psychology: psychotherapy and personality* edited by A.W. Landfield and L.M. Leitner.

Finally, the first chapter could not have been written without the insights provided into George Kelly, the man, from a number of ex-students and friends. In particular, we offer our thanks to Rue Cromwell, Brendan Maher, Al Landfield, William Perry, Franz Epting and Esther Cava.

1
The Life of George Kelly

Has anybody here seen Kelly?
K – E – LL – Y
Find him if you can
He's left us all alone – ee – oh
All on our own – ee – oh
Has anybody here seen Kelly?
Find him if you can!
(C.W. Murphy and Will Letters,
'Has anybody here seen Kelly?' 1909)

A Multidimensional Man

That English music-hall song has been used quite often in relation to George Kelly. But the search to paint a portrait of the man for this book makes the song very pertinent – 'find him if you can'!

There is amazingly little written about George Kelly the person. What follows is based on my own, personal, slight knowledge of him; on Kelly's own writings, including the unpublished autobiographical sketch he wrote; but most of all, upon the anecdotes and views of the many ex-students and colleagues of his who replied to my request for an account of their experiences of and with George Kelly the person.[1]

George Kelly was a man of contrasts. 'A wonderful husband and father' to his wife, Gladys; a fearsome, arrogant or simply unkind figure to some of his ex-students; or one of a small number of 'true', great teachers. To many, including myself, he was a man of great kindness, with an extraordinary ability to read non-verbal cues; a talented actor and someone who tried his hand at poetry and the drawing of cartoons; and a man who, on occasion, could behave in an astonishingly adolescent manner.

He is acknowledged as having been a man of vast creative intellect – a genius, in the opinion of many – as well as a man who seemed to make a cult of never letting anything of 'himself' emerge. On this last point, he apparently instructed his wife to destroy all

... temporarily restoring his secondary
sex characteristics with corresponding
rejuvenescence!

Figure 1 *Drawing from George Kelly's unpublished manuscript, 'Understandable Psychology', 1932*

his personal correspondence and papers. It is said this was because he did not think something that referred to a third party should be made public without their consent. Others think he just did not want to be 'known'.

He is said to have built a house for himself and his family mostly with his own hands. Don Bannister commented on the professional look of his mortise and tenon joints!

He had a very apparent sense of humour (some have called it a 'caustic wit'). This comes through clearly in his essays (see Maher, 1969). He used this to effect in his sketches and some of his poetry. Figures 1 and 2 were amongst several cartoons drawn for a book he wrote called 'Understandable Psychology'. The book was never published but is dated 1932. Figure 1 is a sketch accompanying a discussion of transplants and the endocrine glands. Figure 2 relates to his discussion of 'the second great psychological problem: "How does a person know?"' He explains that problem to his readers thus:

Figure 2 *Drawing from George Kelly's unpublished manuscript, 'Understandable Psychology', 1932*

> At the moment you are undergoing an experience! That mass of physical matter which is *you* is becoming aware of the meaning of these printed lines. How in the world is it done?
>
> 'Why!' you reply, 'I *look* at this printed page, I *see* those black symbols there, and *know* what they mean'.
>
> Yes, that analysis is essentially correct, and the whole process is a process of cognition and comprises an experience. (Kelly, 1932: 34)

The Evidence and its Interpretation

One issue arising from this search for George Kelly concerns the present-day fashion of focusing on the warts rather than the achievements of those who have done unusual things. I am not referring to those who have given me accounts of their personal, sometimes negative, experiencing of George Kelly for this chapter. I am talking about those like myself who try to make sense of another person. This is often done, as in this case, with very little direct evidence and, unlike in psychotherapy, without direct access to that person for corroboration.

My personal belief is that we need to take a person from their own standpoint. What does that person think they are doing *in their own terms*? They need to be assessed as people who lived at a certain point in time, in a certain culture, and with a certain personal history. Warts are part of the complexity of each human being. Strip an adult and you will find a wart or two – particularly on the great. Turned on its head, would great men and women be great if we had managed to give them psychotherapy and succeeded in removing the warts?

So my plan is to follow the modern philosophical view of human beings and to use the dialectic, which is so much a part of personal construct theory. I do not focus on all the warts at the expense of the strengths, nor on all the strengths ignoring the warts, but on a synthesis, viewing George Kelly as a fragmented and contradictory human being who may well not have a single, coherent identity.

It is my intention to try to understand him as best I can from the evidence available to me and not to judge him. To put it in William Perry's words, 'the question is not "Who was George Kelly?" But rather "Who did George Kelly think he was?"'

This chapter is an attempt to describe George Kelly's life, what people say about him, and what he says about himself. That, in turn, is related to aspects of his theory and philosophy as seems relevant. Lastly, in a truly reflexive mode, I look at what I have gleaned about him 'as if' it were the case history of a new psychotherapy client and come up with *my own* transitive diagnosis. It is 'transitive' in the sense that it is to do with transitions in George Kelly's life and, as he himself says, 'We are looking for bridges between the client's present and his future' (Kelly, 1991, Vol. 2: 153). As the client changes so may the transitive diagnoses. Thus, I make my first transitive diagnosis on the evidence available in the full knowledge that it will be superseded by another that will be a better fit as new information becomes available.

I am very conscious of the fact that a psychotherapist will normally only accept a client for psychotherapy if that client wishes it. Would George Kelly have wished this intrusion into his privacy? I do not know. He did write his own autobiographical sketch, and his own 'autobiography of a theory', and allowed people to have copies of his paper 'Confusion and the clock' (Kelly, 1978) even though 'it is more autobiographical than I meant it to be' (Kelly, 1966). One other piece of evidence suggests that he was expecting some such invasion of his privacy as this to take place. Al Landfield mentions an important letter Kelly wrote to Neil Warren after he had been over to England to give a talk at Brunel University in 1964 (Kelly, 1969f). This letter has now disappeared, but Al Landfield remembers Kelly saying in it that he would agree to its being published after his death.

In the final analysis, I sense that George Kelly would have been ambivalent. I can but try to do justice to a man acknowledged to have been great and to have exerted a profound influence on the many people he and his ideas have touched.

Kelly's Early Life and Education

In an unpublished and undated autobiographical sketch,[2] Kelly has this to say about himself:

> I was born on a farm near Perth, Kansas on April 28 1905, the only child of Theodore Vincent Kelly and Elfleda Merriam Kelly. My father had been educated for the Presbyterian ministry at Parsons College and at McCormick and Princeton Seminaries. My mother had been born on Barbados in the British West Indies where her father had taken his family after steam had driven his sailing ship out of the North Atlantic trade. Later Captain Merriam had become an Indian agent in South Dakota and it was at the border town of Brown's Valley, Minnesota that my parents had met. Not long after their marriage the career in the ministry was abandoned and the young couple moved to the farm where I was born.

Don Bannister describes this farm in Kansas thus:

> I took a 200-mile detour to visit Perth, Kansas, and I'm not actually sure I visited it. The signpost said, 'Perth 7 miles'. So I set the odometer on the car and I was in the middle of this vast kind of billiard table. And I passed a cemetery that had quite a few gravestones in it, so there must have been something there at some time, but it had long gone. There was a farm in the distance, and I passed about four more en route. But in England we just never see that amount of space with nothing much in it . . . Someone had been telling me about Sartre, and they were telling me he grew up in Paris, and he looked out over the vast view of roofs, and houses, and tenements, and people crowded in piles. And I did suddenly get a sense of contrast, that, stuck out there on a farm in Kansas, if you didn't *imagine* something, then there wouldn't be much there. You'd have to make something out of it. (Bannister, 1979, personal communication in Neimeyer, 1985a, p. 11)

It is not difficult to see how the child George Kelly had the opportunity to develop his powers of imaginative thought, his vision and curiosity about what lay over the horizon. It is also not difficult to see how he may have been ready to see the world as full of alternatives when we read the part of his autobiographical sketch relating to his educational history. He starts at the age of four:

> In 1909 my father converted our lumber wagon into a covered wagon and moved the family to Eastern Colorado to take up a claim on some of the last free land offered settlers in the west. The venture failed

> because no water could be found under the land, and my parents moved back to the farm in Kansas.
>
> My schooling was rather irregular and in Colorado was limited to the occasions when my parents could spend a few weeks in town. However, since they themselves were educated, they took seriously their responsibility for my studies at home.
>
> My high school education was about as badly mixed up as my elementary schooling had been. After a few weeks commuting to a local high school it was decided to send me to Wichita. Thus it was that I lived away from home most of the time after I was thirteen, and I attended four different high schools.

It would seem likely from this that his whole process of socialization plus the opportunity to build lasting relationships (except with his parents) were seriously impaired. With few peers to play with and other adults to relate to, it would not be surprising if this gifted child stretched his world in imagination to and over the horizon.

However, we do know of another, possibly important, adult in his world: a grandfather who was a captain on sailing ships trading in the North Atlantic. What tales of this wide, exciting world did this grandfather recount to the child? His own ship apparently actually burned. Did the young Kelly hear tales such as those told by Conrad? How ships are loved and cared for and treated as if they were people?

> Yes, your ship wants to be humoured with knowledge. You must treat with an understanding consideration the mysteries of her feminine nature, and then she will stand by you faithfully in the unceasing struggle with forces wherein defeat is no shame. It is a serious relation, that in which a man stands to his ship. She has her rights as though she could breathe and speak; and, indeed, there are ships that, for the right man, will do anything but speak, as the saying goes. (Conrad, 1906: 56)

Evidence that Kelly's sea-faring grandfather may well have told him such exciting tales comes from his paper 'Confusion and the clock', written soon after he had had a heart attack. He writes:

> And I thought of our first grandchild, expected in a few weeks, whom I might never see, and to whom I might never tell the wonderful stories that all grandchildren should hear. (Kelly, 1978: 226)

Further evidence of the influence of this third adult in Kelly's life comes from the many sailing metaphors and analogies Kelly uses in his writings. For instance, he uses the metaphor of navigation to exemplify how prediction works as stated in his fundamental postulate 'A person's processes are psychologically channelized by the ways in which he anticipates events'. He explains what it is that is anticipated or predicted as follows:

> A navigator who has never been to the North Pole may yet know its coordinates so well that he can predict the event of his arrival there. In a sense he does not conjure up the event itself, but rather its properties. Sure enough, twenty-nine days after he makes his prediction he does experience an event having all the predicted properties – time, declination of the sun, and so on – all occurring in conjunction with each other. With this evidence of the converging properties of time and space, he shouts to his companions, 'Here we are; this is it!' His prediction is satisfactorily confirmed.
>
> Let us make sure that we are explicit about this. What one predicts is not a fully fleshed-out event, but simply the common intersect of a certain set of properties. (Kelly, 1991, Vol. 1: 85)

The Graduate Years

Having attended four different high schools, Kelly continues his description of his education as follows:

> When I was sixteen I transferred to the Friends University academy in Wichita and began taking a combination of college and academy courses. Thus it was that I did not actually graduate from high school. A fact that is sometimes hard to explain.
>
> In 1926, after three years at Friends University and one at Park College, Missouri, I completed my baccalaureate studies with majors in physics and mathematics.

His study of physics and mathematics had, I have argued (Fransella, 1983), a profound influence on personal construct theory. At the time Kelly was learning physics, Einstein and those supporting the ideas embodied in quantum mechanics were offering an alternative to the physics of Newton, which had been followed up until then. The so-called 'new' physics argued, amongst other things, that it was not possible to gain access to reality. We do not have direct access to 'the truth'. Here is a clear connection with Kelly's philosophy of constructive alternativism – 'there are always alternative ways of looking at any event' (see p. 13 below). Al Landfield tells how Paula Golden, a physicist who later became a social psychologist, 'commented in my PCP seminar that Kelly's theory can be seen as a good theory of physics'.

The Postgraduate Years

Kelly's autobiography continues by telling us how he moved from being an undergraduate in physics and mathematics to teaching psychology and speech.

> My plan had always been to complete an engineering course after graduating from college, but an interest and some success in inter-collegiate debate aroused my interest in social issues and made me question the ultimate value of a career in engineering. The next fall therefore I enrolled in educational sociology at the University of Kansas, with minor studies in labor relations and sociology. My master's thesis was a study of Kansas City workers' distribution of leisure time activities.
>
> In the fall of 1927, with my thesis still incomplete and no offers of a teaching job, in spite of many applications, I went to Minneapolis. There I managed to survive by teaching one night a week in each of three night-schools: one for the American Bankers Association, one a speech class for labor organizers, and one an Americanization class for prospective citizens. I enrolled in the University of Minnesota in sociology and biometrics, but after several weeks it was discovered that I had been unable to pay my fees and I was told that I could no longer attend.

After getting his MA in 1927 with a thesis on 'One thousand workers and their leisure', he continues thus:

> In the late winter of 1927–28 I was given a job teaching psychology and speech, including the coaching of dramatics, in the Sheldon Junior College at Sheldon, Iowa. The college, then in its second year, had had disciplinary problems and the previous teacher had been run out of town by the rowdy students. The superintendent of schools apparently decided that academic qualifications were of secondary importance and employed me.

One can only wonder what qualities George Kelly was seen to possess that suggested he might be able to deal with these disciplinary problems. It can be assumed that by the age of twenty-two he had a perceived ability to control students.

In this section about Sheldon Junior College, Kelly states he was now well into drama and speech. It is therefore not surprising to find that role play and enactment have a major part in his therapy approach and the methods are central to the one specific therapeutic method he describes – 'fixed role therapy'. It will also be suggested later that a 'fixed role' Kelly wrote for himself played a prominent part in creating George Kelly the man as experienced by some others.

He finishes the educational picture as follows:

> After a year and a half there, a summer in sociology at the University of Minnesota, and a few months as an aeronautical engineer for the struggling Watkins Aircraft Company back in Wichita, responsible for stress analysis, I went to Edinburgh on an exchange fellowship.

In the next few years he got a BEd at Edinburgh University and a PhD in psychology at Iowa University. His dissertation for the former was on predicting teaching success and the latter on 'Common factors in reading and speech disabilities'. Two days after receiving his PhD he married Gladys Thompson.

The Professional Years

After this period he tells us about his first job.

> In the fall of 1931 we set out for Hays, Kansas to teach in the Fort Hays Kansas State College for what was to stretch out into twelve years. It was here that I found there was little occasion to pursue work in physiological psychology and I turned to the kind of psychological services that seemed to be most needed. This was clinical psychology, especially in the schools of the State. Soon we received some legislative support for a program of traveling clinics that gave my students and me a chance to develop our psychological thinking in close contact with persons in distress.

It must have been in the early days at Fort Hays, or some time before, that Kelly wrote his psychology textbook 'Understandable Psychology' (unpublished and dated 1932).

Rue Cromwell talks of how Kelly called Fort Hays 'the hinterlands', and of how, as the 'new boy', Kelly was given the job of testing the incoming students for selection purposes.

> With that mischievous smile and glint in his eye, Kelly would tell us of examining the scores year by year, spotting the top scorers, calling them into his office and saying to them, 'Guess what? You are going to major in psychology.' He would then name the outstanding figures in psychology he had recruited in this way.

The 'glint in the eye' or some such phrase occurs often in the stories sent to me. It always seems to be related to an occasion in which Kelly could be seen as 'bucking' or 'using' or 'challenging' the system.

It was at Fort Hays that Kelly began to exert his influence on psychology. He developed a clinical programme for the psychological evaluation of school-aged children and adults on the campus. These included psychotherapy, vocational and academic counselling, academic skill development and speech therapy.

From this there developed a demand for services in the community. The resulting travelling clinic in rural Kansas became a model on which much future rural school psychology was based. It offered mainly diagnostic and consultative services. At the time Kelly had no staff for this travelling clinic. It was just he and four or five undergraduate and postgraduate students.

Cleanthous et al. (1982) discuss an important document stemming from this time. This was the 'Handbook of Clinic Practice' (Kelly, 1936). It began as a document for students and was continually re-written. It contained 'the Rules' for those working in the clinic. These Rules included a set of ethical statements that are said to be very similar to those currently adopted by the American Psychological Association.

Time was of the essence in the travelling clinic. The aim was to see and evaluate twelve children in a day. This time pressure, combined with Kelly's interest in both the measurement and change of attitudes, resulted in the development of a five-point bi-polar set of rating scales (Jackson et al., 1982). The 'Handbook' therefore shows that Kelly was using 5-point bi-polar rating scales well before 1936. This pre-dates Osgood et al.'s reported work on the Semantic Differential (1957) by more than twenty years. Importantly for the study of the development of Kelly's ideas, this bi-polar format is one commonly used today in repertory grid measurement known as 'the ratings repertory grid'. Also, it shows the early development of the importance he placed on the dialectic. It is a precursor of the Dichotomy Corollary in personal construct theory: 'a person's construction system is composed of a finite number of dichotomous constructs'.

Somehow, while writing the 'Handbook', developing this rural school psychology service and supervising the work of many postgraduate students, Kelly found time to draft a book with W. G. Warnock on 'Inductive Trigonometry' (Kelly and Warnock, 1935). They describe it as a 'textbook, workbook, diagnostic tests, and remedial exercises in trigonometry'. Browsing through the copy I have of this text, I see it as the forerunner of programmed texts that became so popular decades later. The book was never published.

In his 'The autobiography of a theory' (1969a), Kelly describes how, in his early work in Fort Hays in the depression of the 1930s, he had to deal with people who had real problems of daily living, and how he found Freudian interpretations worked with some. But later, he says, he found that his own interpretations also worked provided they a) were relevant to the problem and b) showed the person an alternative way of looking at the problem. Here can be seen the development of his philosophy of *constructive alternativism* and the only major approach to therapy that he described – fixed role therapy. In his 1955 work (1955a), Kelly cites two early theses that were carried out during that productive Fort Hays period. They were written in 1939 and 1940 on the subject of the evaluation of fixed role therapy. It is worth noting that Kelly was also involved in speech and drama work at Fort Hays.

He continues his autobiographical account:

> War clouds began to appear on the horizon in the late thirties and I was put in charge of the flight training program allocated to the college by the Civil Aeronautics Administration and I undertook to learn to fly myself. In the fall of 1943 I was commissioned in the U.S. Naval reserve and stationed in the Bureau of Medicine and Surgery.

Rue Cromwell gives us valuable insight into Kelly's work during this period. He tells how Kelly joined one of several groups of naval air psychologists working on methods for selecting naval air cadets. 'It was easy to glean from Kelly's remarks that he came into this group as that unknown psychologist from a college in Kansas that no one had heard of, and left at the end of the war having won the respect of all of them.' The following list of Kelly's publications by the end of the 1945 war demonstrates the range of his talents: *Problems in the aviation training of British Royal Navy Cadets* (report to US Navy, 1944); *Perceptual integration in the design of aircraft instrument panels* (report to Aviation Psychology Branch, Division of Aviation Medicine, Bureau of Medicine and Surgery, US Navy, 1945); and *Design of the critical difference computer. Design computations and specifications for an analog computer* (Special Devices Division, Bureau of Aeronautics, US Navy, 1945).

It is worth considering here the impact on George Kelly of spending up to five years in the services. Some of his work was to do with training. Was it here that he learned more about the importance of discipline? Brendan Maher asks this same question and suggests that this experience, plus his engineer's goal of making things work efficiently, may have made him less tolerant of those who did not do things the way he thought they should be done.

George Kelly spent a year at the University of Maryland before being appointed to a professorship at Ohio State University in 1945 and then Professor and Director of Clinical Psychology in 1946. He stayed at Ohio State University until 1965 when he took up the Distinguished Professorial Chair in Theoretical Psychology at Brandeis University. He was there for a short time until his death in 1967.

The Man and his Work

The Publication of The Psychology of Personal Constructs

It is difficult to know precisely when Kelly started work on *The Psychology of Personal Constructs*, which was published in 1955. But it seems as if it must have been some time in the 1930s, although his revolutionary ideas no doubt were germinating even before then.

It is the view of Brendan Maher that, with the publication of personal construct theory in 1955, life changed for George Kelly. He became widely known and his presence was in demand all over the world. Maher has this to say about the publication of Kelly's *magnum opus*:

> As far as I can tell George did not contact any publisher at all, and at times it seemed as though the manuscript was something between a possible book and a very long working paper. When it was finally finished, it was typed up on the purple-inked 'ditto' paper that was then used to make copies. Twelve copies were made, packaged and addressed to leading publishers (without any advance warning to them, I believe) and taken to the Post Office by George and some students in George's station-wagon.
>
> Not long after that I happened to have an appointment with him about something. When I entered his office he was sitting at his desk looking genuinely amazed, and pleased. Some publisher's contracts lay on his desk. Not only was the book going to be published – he had a choice of publishers. He expressed his delight, and his surprise, and I do suspect that if the book had been rejected by all twelve, he would not have been entirely surprised.
>
> In George's career there was something of the triumph of the tortoise over the hare. For a long time few people outside professional clinical psychology knew of his work. He had published few articles, and was not a regular performer at conventions and conferences. I think that the response to George's book came as a surprise to some of his colleagues as well as to George himself.

Kelly was certainly ambivalent about the publication of his work. He told me that it was the only one of the five books he had written to be published, and that that might have been a mistake (Kelly, 1966). One suggestion is that he felt it was too early for his radical ideas to be accepted by psychologists. Others felt that he took a rather cavalier attitude towards this work. But there is evidence that Kelly was passionately committed to his theory. Al Landfield says that after reading the missing letter Kelly wrote to Neil Warren in 1964, 'I knew beyond a shadow of a doubt that Kelly's hopes for the theory went way beyond ordinary ambition. His hopes went beyond himself, I believe.' The letter also showed that he 'had a great respect for British scholarship and apparently felt that his theory would sink or swim in British waters. In other words, if British scholars took to his theory, then the theory had a chance in the larger world of science.' I believe Kelly would have been pleased to know his prophecy has largely been borne out, much of this being due to the activities of Don Bannister.

One might think that writing this two-volume theory would have been enough work during the preceding ten years or so, not to mention having a fairly demanding job. But he also managed to carry out research and to write extensively on the effects of television in the classroom in the late 1940s and early 1950s. There was the 'plan' (Kelly, 1953a) and the 'Report on classroom television' written with Lawrence Conrad in 1954. There is also another manuscript, 'Television at the Classroom Door' (Kelly, 1955b). All are unpublished.

Breadth of Vision: Like Man, Like Theory

It is hard not to speculate that his philosophy of *constructive alternativism*, and the importance Kelly attached to the dialectic, stem from his early home life and chequered education. Its breadth of vision is clear and was quite unlike anything in psychology in those years up to the 1950s. This is how he summarizes his philosophy of *constructive alternativism*:

> Like other theories, the psychology of personal constructs is the implementation of a philosophical assumption. In this case the assumption is that whatever nature may be, or howsoever the quest for truth will turn out in the end, the events we face today are subject to as great a variety of constructions as our wits will enable us to contrive. This is not to say that one construction is as good as any other, *nor is it to deny that at some infinite point in time human vision will behold reality out to the utmost reaches of existence*. But it does remind us that all our present perceptions are open to question and reconsideration, and it does broadly suggest that even the most obvious occurrences of everyday life might appear utterly transformed if we were inventive enough to construe them differently. (Kelly, 1970a: 1; italics mine)

He goes further with his audacious thinking – audacious, that is, to much of the psychological world at the time:

> The universe that we presume exists has another important characteristic: it is integral. By that we mean it functions as a single unit with all its imaginable parts having an exact relationship to each other. This may, at first, seem a little implausible, since ordinarily it would appear that there is a closer relationship between the motion of my fingers and the action of the typewriter keys than there is, say, between either of them and the price of yak milk in Tibet . . . A simple way of saying this is to state that *time provides the ultimate bond in all relationships*. (1991, Vol. 1: 5; italics in original)

William Perry comments that 'the vision he put forward impressed me so deeply, was so far-reaching, so futuristic, that I had a sense of dealing with a new scripture'.

Another ex-student, Denny Hinkle (1970), tells of his conversation with George Kelly about his theory in a chapter entitled 'The game of personal constructs':

> 'Seek to understand a man's questions, not simply his answers' advised George Kelly. And when I asked what questions he was exploring by writing 'The Psychology of Personal Constructs' he said – with that twinkle of aggressive enthusiasm (fr. *entheos* – the god within – divine inspiration) – 'American psychologists have seemed like such a sorry lot; imagine being that cut off from an understanding of the wonder of people and the truth of human relationships! I wondered in writing construct theory if I could devise a way to help them discover people and yet still feel scientifically respectable in doing that'. In 1966 I asked him how he would have changed those two volumes, now that he had the perspective of over a decade later. After indicating that he probably would delete the section on the repgrid, because it seemed to him that methodologically-oriented researchers had let it obscure the contribution of the theory, he added wistfully 'At the time I was already concerned that it might be too far from the mainstream to be recognized as psychology, but now – yes – I think I would have written it more honestly'.
>
> More *honestly*? And what was he getting at when he said (G.A. Kelly, personal communication):
>
> '. . . I imagine a society truly based on psychology – a society in which each person's experience, creativity and human relationships are the central issues'.
>
> And finally:
>
> 'Personal Construct Theory is fundamentally a theory of human action'.
>
> These have been bits of a fascinating puzzle about the questions of a great man. They have also been the points of departure for this essay and the lands at the outreach of the magical Personal Construct Theory telescope – with kaleidoscopic attachment! (Hinkle, 1970: 91)

It is not relevant to the purpose of this book to follow Hinkle's discussion of these points, but they do provide some insight into Kelly's own thinking. For instance, that passage about Kelly feeling that psychologists were cut off from the 'understanding of the wonder of people and the truth of human relationships!' It could be and has been argued here that Kelly was recognizing some issues of his own in relating to people and that part of the drive in his creation of personal construct theory was to elaborate his own construing. He did, after all, say that a theory will always reflect the construing of its creator.

Kelly is also known to have been very ambivalent about the repertory grid and his belief that it obscured the theory. I suggested that he was wrong in this belief since several people, including myself, had come to the theory having first encountered his work through the grid.

Miller Mair discusses Kelly's vision further:

> The kind of venture which seems to me to assume a central place in personal construct psychology is not the 'big game hunting' or 'conquering Everest' variety. It is something both more homey and more audacious. What Kelly seems to be advocating is something like 'life on the frontier' – living on the frontiers of your experience rather than within cosily settled conventions or as a more-or-less victim of the demands of tradition. You can almost hear the 'wagon trains moving westward' seeking new pastures and more space for living, as you read Kelly's writings. (Mair, 1977: 268)

George Kelly's young world had included the tales of large ships sailing a vast ocean, bounded only by the horizon, where people experienced loves and hates, had exciting adventures and probably some fearful moments also. But there was also the isolated farm in a vast plain bounded only by the horizon. On that plain he would watch the sun rise as he milked the farm's cows. Perhaps 'the truth', life, knowledge, was always just over that horizon? It is not so much 'life on the frontier' but 'life on or beyond the horizon'. Kelly suggests as much himself when talking about finding answers:

> In the world of unknowns seek experience, and seek it full cycle. That is to say, if you go ahead and involve yourself . . . if you dare to commit yourself, if you prepare to assess the outcomes as systematically as you can, and if you master the courage to abandon your favourite psychologisms and intellectualisms and reconstrue life altogether; well, you may not find that you guessed right, but you will stand a chance of transcending more freely those 'obvious' facts that now appear to determine your affairs, and you just may get a little closer to the truth that lies somewhere over the horizon. (Kelly, 1977: 19)

Construing is a Bi-Polar Activity

We know that Kelly was using scales involving polar adjectives in the early 1930s. The task here is to see whether there is any evidence from his past that might lead us to predict such interest. Perhaps he observed this pull of opposites within his own life.

It is as if there were two George Kellys. There is the Kelly with the great breadth of vision as exhibited in his philosophy, and the Kelly who had an almost obsessive concern for detail. This is reflected in the two-fold structure of his theory. On the one hand, it gives a skeletal account of how a person may go about the business of making sense of current events and predicting future events; all expounded in great and sometimes monotonous detail. On the other hand, it also gives an account of human experiencing or – as he planned to entitle a book which he never completed – it is about 'The Human Feeling' (Kelly, 1966).

Turned into a construct it becomes *breadth of vision* versus *attention to detail.*

It is difficult to know precisely where George Kelly's desire for detail comes from. Perhaps from his Presbyterian father? One of the few comments I have about his father is in a personal letter to me in which he was discussing antiques. He says:

> This past week I have been packing and crating articles in my workshop. Among the articles is an old carpenter's brace with a makeshift block of wood with which my father had replaced the pummel. I remember using it as a youngster on the farm, and of feeling critical of my father because all his tools seemed so crude and patched up – this brace included. But his frugality enabled him to send me to college. (Kelly, 1965)

Perhaps the religious aspect of his upbringing contributed. Certainly Kelly knew his Bible well. He used religious metaphors widely – often to great effect, as is shown later in this chapter. Perhaps he was aware of a need for an anchor after his excursions into the world of imagination. Whatever the reason, we do have here an account of what later became the *creativity cycle.* This is the constant flow between the joy of creation and the rigour and commitment of action.

The Influence of Science, Mathematics and the Role of Commitment

Apart from its influence on the philosophical underpinnings of personal construct theory, his training in physics and mathematics led to his explicit creation of the sort of person he saw us all as being. The person is a scientist, doing the sorts of things scientists do.

Looking at the person 'as if' he or she is a scientist leads to two radical ingredients of his theory. The person conducts his or her own personal experiments to test out their construing of events. We test hypotheses in true scientific style. But the test we use is our own behaviour. Behaviour becomes our personal experiment. More on this later.

An additional, essential feature of 'the person as scientist' is commitment. You cannot conduct these personal experiments without first committing yourself to them. That is all spelled out in Kelly's 'cycle of experience'. He relates commitment to psychological research. Just being involved in an experiment is not enough:

> There is commitment. The human venture is not an exercise in passive receptivity, nor is understanding developed out of sensory experience

> alone. As for the child who must manipulate the world in his mouth or with his ever-moving hands, so for the psychologist, too, who comes to know man only by doing something with men. So he commits himself to a human course of action. Without doing so he can never know what relevance his own construction of life has to the lives that others live.
>
> Commitment, I fully realise, means aggression – personal aggression – and if the outcome brings a sense of having violated his role, the psychologist will experience guilt. Thus commitment can never be undertaken without risking one's virtue and sometimes losing it, nor without the possibility of emerging as a villain and sometimes actually doing just that. So in undertaking commitment the strategy of psychological research requires one to take deep personal risks. No wonder so many of us would like to become scientists and be content to win prizes without having to take an awful responsibility for people. (Kelly, 1969f: 130)

There is little doubt that this commitment seen as part of 'the person as scientist' is very much part of George Kelly the person. Evidence comes from Brendan Maher when talking about Kelly's contribution to clinical psychology and his commitment to its professional independence.

> George had been very active as a member of the group that had planned and conducted the 'Boulder Conference' in which a general standard for training in clinical psychology had been developed and accepted by the doctoral clinical programs in all of the major US universities. The Boulder Model, as it came to be known . . . [placed] a strong emphasis upon issues of professional ethics, professional behavior, and a belief in the wisdom of the complete professional independence of clinical psychologists, i.e. the removal of the legal requirement that the activities of clinical psychologists be supervised by psychiatrists (in some States the requirement was simply that the supervisor be a physician – with no need for psychiatric qualifications!) . . . In this matter a large group of senior clinical psychologists (including George Kelly) . . . combined to found the American Board of Examiners in Professional Psychology (ABEPP). This was (and still is) a non-statutory body designed to create high standards of practice, to conduct practical examinations and to award diplomas to the successful candidates – who were required to have the PhD in clinical psychology, plus the equivalent of at least two years of full-time post-PhD clinical experience. George was one of the central figures in the ABEPP, and was frequently sought out by them and by the APA as a consultant on matters of alleged ethical violations by members.

Maher goes on to provide a link between commitment and role play.

Talent as an Actor, Non-Verbal Construing, and Role Play

Kelly's interest and involvement in acting led him to study Moreno's development of psychodrama (for example, Moreno,

1964). This, in turn, could be seen in his use of role play in everyday life. He appears to have consciously played parts, often that of 'the conventional professor', and he used his behaviour to make a particular point. Brendan Maher talks of his having 'on-stage' and 'off-stage' roles, the 'on-stage' roles helping him deal with the many differing responsibilities professors had to undertake. Kelly's commitment to these responsibilities sometimes led him to behave in ways that made him unpopular. For instance, Brendan Maher talks of students who were seen to be ill-equipped for their hoped-for career in clinical psychology:

> George felt a responsibility for both the marginal student and to the future potential client, and when the facts were clear was willing to take the necessary action. To some people this appeared heartless. However, when I returned to Ohio State as a faculty member in 1955 and participated in meetings of the clinical faculty, it was obvious that the other senior faculty spontaneously identified the unsuitable student as unsuitable, but would always turn to George to do the unpleasant task of informing the student. As long as George was Director of Clinical Training he felt that he should accept that responsibility. The inevitable result was that George would become the target of the hostility of the student and his or her friends, the student even receiving expressions of sympathy from the same members of the faculty who had been urging the dismissal of the student in the private meeting of the day before.

An example of how George Kelly used role play when it came to the task of dismissing students is given by Rue Cromwell. He says he is not sure this actually happened, but students believed it did and that is what mattered:

> As the story goes, there were a number of students in the clinical psychology program, left over from the previous directorship, who were judged unfit to continue. One day Kelly arrived at work in bib overalls and a blue farmer's workshirt. He called the students in one by one and dismissed them from the clinical psychology training program. Sometime along the way he remarked casually that when you have to clean the manure out of the barn you must be dressed for the task . . . this story certainly recapitulates many of the elements and features of Kelly, including the awe and fear with which he was held during my era at Ohio State University.

But Cromwell goes on to say:

> My message here, however, is that I feel that what we are and have today in clinical psychology, especially in the USA, rests greatly upon the pristine caretaker attitudes of Kelly and his generation. The harsh decisions in dealing with students during that time had its benefits – and most clinical psychologists today are without awareness of these benefits; they take it all for granted.

Kelly's commitment was an internal, personal matter which he demonstrated behaviourally rather than verbally. This can be seen either as part of his personal privacy or as a negative characteristic. For example, William Perry says:

> He conspicuously avoided involvement in a rich abundance of campus political issues, even declining to endorse petitions on humanitarian or civil libertarian issues. It is crucial to note in this regard that the '60s saw a torrent of political activity at Ohio State University, including a *horrendous* free-speech-on-campus struggle, which led to (and I use these words advisedly) a *massive exodus* of social science and humanities faculty in the mid-to-late '60s. And, true, Kelly was part of that Great Leave-Taking, but he left *never* having said *anything* publicly. (emphasis is in original)

As with his role play, his response here was behavioural rather than verbal.

The Zeal of the Individualist or of the Rebel?

George Kelly not only created a *revolutionary* theory of how individuals experience and relate to their world but also portrayed the individual in his theory as 'a personal anarchist' (McWilliams, 1988). Kelly describes a psychology of the person which essentially rebels against mainstream behaviourism and the more clinical psychodynamic approach of Freud and his followers. McWilliams uses the metaphor of the personal anarchist in the sense that

> personal insurrection is a personal application of constructive alternativism, for it represents an intentionally aggressive approach to following Kelly's assumption that constructs are revisable and replaceable. The goal is not to destroy the ability to deal effectively with the real world, but to facilitate continuing differentiation and elaboration of personal functioning, to remain fresh and open, perennially ready to deal with moment-to-moment reality in new and effective ways without rigid reliance on pre-existing rules. (McWilliams, 1988: 21)

What evidence is there that George Kelly possessed a rebellious spirit or enjoyed being a rebel? He certainly appears to have enjoyed the revolution going on in physics. But perhaps there are hints earlier than that. Did he, perhaps, choose to be a rebel in his four high schools rather than construe himself as 'an outcast' or 'a misfit' or just 'different'? Did the glint in the eye start here?

Several people have commented on how he used to take great pleasure in recounting his unorthodox educational history to his students. Rue Cromwell says:

> Kelly took great delight in telling us of his nomadic career as a penniless scholar . . . I recall his claiming, with great delight, that he received his

> first statistics – at the University of Minnesota, where he never paid a dime for tuition.

His autobiography shows how he constantly tried to manipulate the system in order to satisfy his obvious thirst for knowledge. Some might say that this behaviour was immoral or 'cheating'. Kelly clearly saw it as evidence of the success of his own wily ways. The way he chose all the top scorers at Fort Hays to major in psychology was, as Rue Cromwell says, 'on the edge of ethics'. He liked to bend or break the rules.

Al Landfield says this of him:

> Kelly was a revolutionary in the guise of a very formal man. Maybe that is why he could be so surprising. There is the story of Kelly suggesting that a disturbed woman might be better off as a high class prostitute.

I have often talked and written along the lines that Kelly indeed had enormous breadth of vision and was a revolutionary thinker. But I also believe he must have been a man of outstanding self confidence, even grandiosity, since he wrote a theory designed to encompass the sum total of human experiencing: something no one else has ever tried to do.

I now find that others think there was an element of grandiosity in George Kelly . Rue Cromwell has this to say about a particular meeting with students:

> After his book was finished and not yet out, he was responding to an apparent criticism of some that he did not cite anyone in the book, did not allow people to see the roots or antecedents of personal construct theory. He jokingly said he was prompted to write an additional chapter entitled 'Apologetics' for the book. Before we saw the humor in his comment, he had to explain to us that apologetics is that branch of theology which deals with the defense and proof of Christianity.

This raises a very important point that needs developing. What was the role of religion in Kelly's thinking?

A Man of Religion

The knowledge that George Kelly was steeped in religious orthodoxy, coupled with a suggested grandiose view of himself in relation to his work, meant I was not surprised to receive William Perry's account of a comment two students, separately, had told him about. Kelly apparently said in a lecture: 'Personal construct theory is God's attempt to put on Man's eyeglasses – to see reality through Man's eyes.'

We know that George Kelly was a practising Christian, extremely familiar with the Bible and religious matters generally and that he was a teetotaller. But he was not rigid in the sense that he wished to impose his own views on others. For instance, Kelly regularly discussed his current writing with a group of students, and Rue Cromwell says:

> Kelly quickly discovered that he would get a better attendance (and perhaps better responsiveness) if there was beer-drinking as a part of the gathering. So, he brought a case of beer each week in his car trunk, and we would meet at one of the students' apartments. Kelly, already having established himself with us as a teetotaller, also brought along a thermos bottle of iced tea for himself.

At Ohio State University he was, says Cromwell, 'an active member of his Church at a time when this was looked upon askance by the (liberal, atheistic, agnostic) faculty in general'. Again, the same theme of going against the tide.

His two volumes (1991) are shot through with examples from the scriptures. The following is from a paper published after his death called 'Sin and psychotherapy'. This also illustrates the folksy style in many of his essays that is in marked contrast to that used in his major work *The Psychology of Personal Constructs*. Towards the end of the paper, Kelly discusses what happens when we look at our responses to those who we claim are guilty of some dark deed:

> The most primitive way to deal with a person who has done something evil is to retaliate. He does something bad, therefore, something bad can be done to him. This makes nearly everybody happy, except, of course, the fellow who starts the trouble. This procedure has two psychological effects: it extends coveted privileges to those who haven't had the nerve to try the same thing, and it serves warning on others who might be similarly tempted to start something.
>
> An incident in the life of Jesus is a case in point. You remember He came upon a group of men about to stone a girl to death. She had been caught in the local parking lot at a rather inconvenient moment in her emotional life. Jesus suggested to the gang that if they really wanted to do it in an orderly fashion the fellow who had never sinned should heave out the first stone. I have the feeling that being the kind of punks they were they all had a pretty specific idea of what he meant, and that none of them wanted to admit in front of the others that he was innocent of that sort of thing – though I suspect some of them might have been innocent in this respect. The upshot was that they decided to give up the project, perhaps to go off and get into some mischief on the other side of town. But up to that point none of the goings on really had much to do with the girl and the sin she had committed. (Kelly, 1969b: 180–1)

He goes on to say that 'Throughout our culture it is pretty generally believed that behavior is controlled by red and green lights, known as punishment and rewards' (Kelly, 1969b: 182). He then extends this to religion:

> And the same game is played under theological rules. Man makes a mistake. That upsets the Almighty. There is disagreement on just how it upsets Him. Some say it makes Him furious and others say that it depresses Him. Whichever it is, it is up to man to do something to restore the Almighty's peace of mind. So man punishes himself or whoever it was who made the mistake. The Almighty wholeheartedly approves of this, and it makes Him feel so warm and permissive that He is disposed to forget the whole thing. He may even offer to pick up the tab for the damages caused by the sinful act. Under these theological rules man plays the classical role of a court fool in the Kingdom of Heaven. (Kelly 1969b: 182)

Rue Cromwell asks: 'Is this to be viewed as a rebellion against his somewhat fundamentalistic teetotalling father? Or did his father and he share a spark of intellectual and religious thinking about the underlying mythologic structure of religion?'

When I asked Al Landfield whether he saw a relationship between Kelly's religion and his theory, he replied:

> Yes, indeed, I believe that Kelly perceived the relevance of his theory to faith and religion . . . but certainly not a literal kind of religion. I remember Kelly saying, and I cannot recapture the context, that science and religion were two ways of stretching out and making sense of the universe. Kelly saw that changes and developments could occur in religion just as in science.

Perhaps Kelly sought the same fusion of science and religion as Einstein who said 'science without religion is lame, religion without science is blind' (quoted in Frank, 1947: 285). In reply to my question about whether Kelly was indeed a deeply religions man Al Landfield says:

> I think so. However, his religion was not dogma. I think he saw the mainspring of life as a creative search and a stretching out and a stretching inward. He, I think, respected both creative science and creative religion. Yet, I think that he was not ready to become a great political leader for science or religion. Note that he did not push his theory the way some academics do, for fame and recognition. Kelly seemed to believe in slow change. Great ideas grow slowly. Did he know this truth or was he essentially introvertive, or fearful of his own grandiosity? Maybe both.

Grandiosity comes up once again. Landfield spoke of a paper by MacKinnon (1962) describing his work on 'genius'. One conclusion was that highly creative people tend to feel secretly that they may have some key to the universe. It may not be too far-fetched to believe this of George Kelly too.

Kelly and Social Interaction

Having looked at how George Kelly's personal history may have influenced not only him but also his theory, it is now time to look more closely at George Kelly the man as experienced by others.

It occurs to me that there are at least three aspects of George Kelly to be looked at. First, there seem clearly to have been two George Kellys who engaged in social relationships – the rule-bound person and the fun-loving, creative person – and he could switch from one to the other at a moment's notice. Second, there are marked differences in how he behaved towards, and was perceived by, different groups of his students. Third, he is seen to have been uncomfortable with social interactions that required some expression of emotional involvement.

Social Relationships

An essential feature of social relationships in personal construct theory is the idea of *role*. We are said to play a role in relation to others if we try to see things through the eyes of that other person. The psychotherapist is a supreme example of the Kellyian role player.

Kelly is certainly seen by many of my informants as sometimes having difficulty in understanding the positions of others. Al Landfield says:

> I think he felt barriers between himself and others. Maybe these barriers relate to his being an only child brought up in considerable isolation. It also is possible that he may have perceived a gulf between his intellect that was formidable and that of many others. Perhaps he needed to understand others (sociality corollary) because he knew others would have difficulty understanding him.

One aspect of his behaviour that comes over clearly from all who have been kind enough to send me comments and anecdotes is his insistence on 'professional' dress and rule-bound behaviour. Everyone has mentioned the fact that Kelly insisted on students calling him 'Professor' and on his calling them 'Mister', 'Miss' or 'Mrs' – right up to the acceptance of their PhD dissertation. From that minute it was 'George', and he called them by their first names.

A story sometimes discussed among the graduate students is relevant here. It is said that Kelly wrote a fixed role sketch for himself. He would not let anyone else get involved in it. Normally the therapist sketches the fixed role for the client to adopt for a period of time, but it is always with the acceptance of the client that this is a reasonable person to be. Thus, the writing of a fixed role sketch normally takes a minimum of two people. As someone says, Kelly broke his own rule and that the fixed role therapy that he performed on himself may have been responsible for 'the very personally conservative man that we all knew . . . Freud as you know analysed himself. He would allow no one else to do that. Kelly could have made the same mistake. How "personally" afraid they both were of letting others know much about them.'

The total opposite of the formal, rule-bound person was the intellectually excited, creative person who came over as very warm and interested. It is not surprising that ideas could catch the attention of this brilliant man. For instance, when Kelly was on a visit to England, he and Don Bannister (who also loved playing with ideas) arrived on my door-step just after midnight. Having carelessly run out of coffee, I offered drinking chocolate. Around the fire they started challenging each other, ending with designing a course on 'a psychology of serendipity'. I only wish I had had a tape-recorder running.

I had personal experience of this combination of the two George Kellys when I was visiting the United States. Having collected me at the airport, he took me to Brandeis University where all his PhD students were gathered around a large table. Having been supplied with coffee, I had the task of talking to them about my ideas and work with those who stutter. At some point I became aware of one of those awful silences which suggest you have done or said something terrible. I looked toward George Kelly at the end of the table. He said, with that glint in his eye: 'How do you like the English coffee?' I was about to say something to the effect that it was particularly nice, when it suddenly dawned on me that it was drinking chocolate! He had apparently burned out two coffee percolators trying to make it!

Part of the problem people say they had with him was that he would switch from the 'warm, excited, involved creator of ideas' to the rigid, rule-bound person and back again so rapidly. Kelly's personal construct name for this is 'slot-rattling'.

Al Landfield gives an example of the radical shifts in mood that could occur:

> I perceived him as most complex. He could suddenly break out of his formality and surprise you.
>
> [His formality] that much exceeded that of other professors, I experienced strongly. However, it broke down on several occasions with me, and in a startling way. When I began to talk with him about my dissertation, he suddenly canceled all appointments for the afternoon. He behaved like a kid with a toy. He interacted with me in a way that cut away all barriers between us. For that afternoon, I felt an equal. Then it

> all changed back again. I was Mr Landfield, in a way that seemed to deny our interaction.

Another ex-student gives the example of how this switching of behaviour caused inter-personal problems in another context. When, just after the publication of *The Psychology of Personal Constructs* in 1955, he asked Kelly for his signature in Volume 1, Kelly wrote:

> To a promising student,
> who, while I'm not sure
> what he actually promises,
> will certainly produce
> something worth-while for
> those whom he touches.

The student comments on how the first line gives, the second two take away and the last three equivocate. 'Another way to say it is the sweet (first line) was often followed by the salty (second two lines) then culminates in the polite. This is what would just drive people mad in trying to relate to Kelly. There was a kind of acceptance and then a rejection which was followed by a kind of politeness which had the appearance often of being passively hostile or passively aggressive.' This type of behaviour caused great problems to some of his students.

Kelly the Teacher

The following excerpt from *A Student's Outline of Graduate Training in Clinical Psychology in the Ohio State University* (1953b) states how Kelly saw his course:

> The training program is also designed to be liberal in the best sense of the term. The coming decades promise many changes in the conceptual frames employed by scientists. The student who is trained as an avowed disciple of *Gestalt Theorie, Nondirectivism* or *Psychoanalysis* is too much in danger of being stuck in his pigeon hole system long after it has lost its usefulness. Not only is the program intended to place more than one conceptual system at the disposal of the student but it is hoped that he can be made free to re-constitute his conceptual system from time to time during his career. Thus, it is planned that teaching will free students' concepts as well as fix them. (Kelly, 1953b: 22)

It has been said that Kelly put his commitment to the development of the profession of clinical psychology before his individual students. We certainly know that he was very committed to his chosen profession. There are such conflicting accounts in this area that it seems reasonable to hypothesize what sort of teacher George

Kelly was. Some ex-students describe him as one of the few 'true' teachers. Brendan Maher says:

> He was undoubtedly one of the small number of true teachers that I have met. He was delighted to hear the student's ideas, to encourage and help the student to bring them to a successful completion. This is the kind of thing that does not make students into mechanical imitators, nor indeed into disciples, in the narrow sense of the word. What it did do was to make many of us feel that he respected us, was willing to have us disagree with him and that he always had at the back of his own head the possibility that he might be wrong; it made us into lifelong friends, admirers of Kelly the man, aware of the possibility of error in our own convictions, and free to pursue our ideas as we saw fit, and know that we were honouring his teaching in doing so.

Others experienced him as being exceptionally uncaring in his treatment of them. I will give some examples of experiences, cited by ex-students, of George Kelly as a teacher, which led to some feeling fear, anxiety or general hostility toward him.

William Perry, for instance, tells about one of his encounters with Kelly:

> In 1963, when I returned to Ohio State from a year's internship in Palo Alto, I came back sporting a spanking-new beard (historically, this period was the freshest blending of the 'beatnik' era and that of the newborn 'hippie' generation). One day soon after my return, in the clinic office at Arps Hall, Professor Jules Rotter was 'giving me attitude' about my goatee when Kelly walked in. Rotter quipped to Kelly, ' I was just stating to Mr Perry' (such appellations, many of us believed, were at Kelly's insistence) 'my opinion that young men with beards are actually rebelling against authority'. Kelly's immediate response was, 'Oh? I would think that young men with beards don't know *how* to rebel against authority'. My sense of this scenario is thus: while Rotter was challenging me, he was inviting a response. Kelly's rejoinder was dismissive, to be taken as the Last Word: I recall his making it over his shoulder, as he walked away.

Kelly apparently often made use of his skills of acting in the form of role play, sometimes to the discomfort of his students. Rue Cromwell gives one example:

> Kelly often used nonverbal behaviour to express his approval or disapproval of ideas. When an idea excited him, he would often suck in a gust of air through his almost closed lips and smile . . . When he disapproved of an idea in a group setting – whether from faculty or student – he would fairly obviously take his glasses off, drop his head as if ashamed of being present, put an ear piece of his glasses in his mouth, then peer upwards (as if above his spectacles) around the room from his bowed position in search of someone whose wisdom he respected, and then smile quietly and knowingly at them as if to say, 'Have you ever in your life heard anything so stupid as that?!' If you were the one he

spotted to make this gesture to, you knew you were 'in'. If you were the one talking at the time this gesture was made, you knew you were in trouble. I believe these dramatic gestures, which I saw repeatedly while working in the Clinic that year, were a carryover from his drama days where he learned the power of such expressions without speech.

Esther Cava gives an example of his disturbing behaviour to her class:

> Despite his very vocal lack of interest in – even rejection of – Freudian psychology, he would seem to derive some pleasure from implications that some deep psychoanalytic pathology was responsible for some of our behaviors. For instance, our class had a seminar with him – some 10 of us – and in front of the class he would slyly remark that there must be some deep-seated Freudian reason why B. P., our only black student, would keep twirling a toothpick in his mouth. We were all embarrassed for B. P. And I was a target for this same implied interpretation brought to the attention of the class for crossing my arms across my chest.

She says that one student commented 'if one were to pull away Kelly's mask one would find Mephistopheles. I guess I felt that way.'

As background information, Esther Cava tells how she and some others were 'directed' to Kelly's class and how angry this had made him. Perhaps it made him angry because he thought that 'the student should exercise considerable initiative in determining what he should study, what he should not study, with whom he should study and with whom he will not study . . .' (Kelly, 1958: 5).

One obvious question is whether or not he was aware of the effect he was having on his students. Rue Cromwell tells a story that suggests Kelly was not reading or not looking for their non-verbal cues. That is, he was not construing their construction processes. Or perhaps he was deliberately ignoring them. But what this and other stories show is Kelly's willingness and ability to change when students made him aware of their discomfort.

> One day during my first or second year at OSU Kelly decided that he would like a group of students together to go to Purdue University and meet their clinical psychology students. Dr Kelly sent word for one of his favorite students to report to his office. He wanted him to contact other students and help organize the trip, but Kelly did not say so in the message. The summoned student, of course, like most of us at the time, interpreted this message to mean that his day had arrived. Consequently, as I was told by others at the time, the student arrived in Dr Kelly's office completely mute from his distress.
>
> This event, as I well recall, had a profound effect on Dr Kelly, who had not fully realized the effect he was having on his students. As has so often been recounted, Kelly went home and re-wrote his own role because of his personal alarm about this. Among the changes in his

> role were a) resign from the position as Director of Clinical Psychology Training, b) move out of the office (the immediate environment where he had dispatched so many students), c) get a coffee pot for his new office and never fail to offer a coffee to any student who came by and stuck his/her head in this door for any reason, d) always keep the door to his office open so that students could see him and he could see students.

Kelly may not always have been aware of the effect his behaviour was having on his students – or he gave no sign that he was. But there is also evidence that his students were equally not always all aware of the effect their behaviour was having on him. This last example of George Kelly's relationship with some of his students comes from those obviously very important regular meetings at which he would read to them his latest draft of a part of his writing. Rue Cromwell recalls them like this:

> With the background of hostility toward Kelly whom we felt still controlled our fates, we often used this opportunity to 'tear his writing to shreds'. I marveled at how he could walk away sometimes dejected . . . and yet return the next week in good spirits and with a re-writing which was not only responsive to our criticisms but which was with such improved quality as to defy another attack . . . .
>
> I cannot resist pointing out that, in spite of my sharp criticism of Kelly's approach with students, these manuscript readings represent to me the very highest that can be achieved in pedagogy: a) Each of us who participated could see some idea or sentence in the book which we personally had helped craft – and Kelly was clearly appreciative and generative with us for our help. It was great for our self esteem and intellectual growth. b) It was a situation where the pedagogue allowed himself to grow along with the student rather than just to 'deliver'.

In an unpublished paper he wrote in 1958 on 'Teacher–student relations at the university level', Kelly talks of this group experience and shows how personally involved he was. He explains how he decided he had to write this book, however it turned out, and how:

> I hated what I wrote; but I was going to write it anyway. I did something else, I invited anybody who wanted, including my students, to come every Thursday evening to listen to me read what I had written during the week and to make comments on it. Now this was a very rugged experience. Sometimes we covered as much as one page of manuscript and sometimes we covered much more. But they forced me to rewrite. Some of them told me that what I had written made no sense at all. They couldn't understand it. Besides, I didn't really believe all that nonsense, they were sure. They enjoyed this and I have never had a stronger group of students come through a program. . . . Some time later, some of the students said, 'Do you know, when you were doing that, (this happened over a three year period, by the way; it was a long torture for me) we would go out together, afterwards, and sit around the table and say

"Now do you think we hit him too hard tonight? Do you think maybe he'll quit writing?"' . . . So then, they would come around to me individually and say 'Now, don't give up just because the rest have criticized. Come on, keep going. I'm on your side.' And then they would usually decide as a group that they would hit me again the next week, until it really looked as if I was going to go down. Then, they would pick me up . . . nearly all of them have their Ph Ds now, as a group, they are very loyal to me and to this experience, and I feel I have colleagues to whom I can go for advice. (Kelly, 1958: 13–14)

To round this off, before moving to the question 'What sort of teacher did George Kelly think he was?', there follows the comment made by Rue Cromwell after I had sent him my 'find' from the unpublished 1958 paper:

Kelly, I remember, did not employ caustic wit in these meetings. He was busy taking notes and trying to understand our criticisms clearly. I look back and think perhaps this was the high point of Kelly's teaching career (except for his written legacy). He challenged us to think. In taking the punishing criticism passively and incorporating our ideas, he gave us an uncommon sense of self esteem, because we realized that OUR OWN ideas were going to appear in a REAL book. And Kelly was generous; he went out of his way to credit people . . .

So, what sort of teacher did George Kelly think he was? There is clear evidence of what he thought a 'bad teacher' was. This comes in the form of a poem he wrote at some unknown time. This poem is entitled 'Nursery rhymes for older tots: to all you kettles, from all us pots'. There is much anger in it against the orthodox teacher. As a person he appeared to many as a very formal man. But his theory is revolutionary and his commitment to teaching is unquestioned. Because it seems important in any attempt to understand what Kelly thought he was doing, the poem is given in full:

Teacher, Teacher – teacher taught,
What you teach is what I ought.
Keep it simple, make it plain;
Big ideas are too much strain.

Mark the pages I must scan;
Read them to me when you can.
Tell me only what I need;
Ask me only what I've seed.

Now add my hours. I made the team,
Got in no scrape, dreamed up no dream.
So graduate me by the rules,
And recommend me to the schools.

Dear Teacher, Teacher, I've been bought,
And, what I teach is what you taught.

An education *I* can claim;
But why were all *your* efforts vain?

******

Teacher, Teacher, you've been taught
Intellectual tommyrot.
Get this straight – if you remain:
You are here to play our game!

Teach the brats to spell and figger,
Snatch their fortunes, bloat them bigger.
Don't talk theoretically;
Make them want things they can see.

Avoid the controversial,
For they must buy what we must sell.
Historic values thus they'll gain,
While strange ideas are never sane.

So Teacher, Teacher, you've been hired
To worship all that we've acquired.
What more in life *is* there to know
Than that what *we* believe is so?

******

Teacher, Teacher – strict upbrought,
Truth is that which you've been taught.
All that contradicts is sin;
Therefore man needs discipline.

Never question any saint;
Question only those who ain't.
Never seek an answer new;
Only answers old are true.

Install a monolithic faith
To guide each step a man may take.
Thus, tuned to your authority,
His life shall run perpetually.

And, Teacher, Teacher . . . orthodox,
Abolish dreams and stop all clocks,
For hopes and hours do *press* us so
We sometimes *question* what we know.

Teacher, Teacher, vainly sought,
Noble skeptic, bold in thought,
Keen assayer of all man's gains,
Where stand you amidst these claims?

Down those halls where pupils learn
Voices, stupid, strident, stern,

Teaching children codes of cowards.
Much too much resemble ours.

Still, you are part of us, the part
Denied when safer lusts our heart
Desired, and in us gaped instead
A dark, where truth is raped by dread.

Teacher, teacher, if our will
To comprehend shall dare not fill
This void in our society,
Then in what sense *can* we be free?

******

Critics, teachers, kettles, pots,
Boobies, bullies, and bigots,
Whilst flushing freedoms down the drain,
Cry, '*Education* is to blame!'

No dreams, no sceptics, and above all freedoms flushed down the drain in this type of teaching. Buried in the unpublished 1958 paper is a statement about how Kelly thought a teacher should be. As one might guess, it is based on the principles of personal construct theory. It also contains the evidence needed to be sure that Kelly was aware of some of his destructive behaviour towards his students – even if not all.

> In high school perhaps you try to control students; you try to get them to do the things they ought to do; you try to get them to wash behind their ears, or to use the dictionary, or to discover the encyclopedia or to read a book that has not been assigned. You try to control them. But in the university the task becomes one of shifting from that, over to challenging them, making them so miserable with their present state of knowledge that out of sheer exasperation with you or with their own ignorance, or with something else, they go out and they find out something. So, the task is to stop controlling and to challenge instead. *But sometimes when we attempt to challenge, we only destroy. Sometimes our efforts to challenge really degenerate into a kind of negative hostile control; and this is of course a pitfall for us.*
>
> Well this is a shift; or to say it in another way, we have to teach our students how to replace certainty with uncertainty. There's a line in the musical play 'The King and I' where it says that people fight most violently for the things they are not quite sure are so, but which they don't want to admit they are questioning. The things that you really feel comfortable about you don't usually get quite so violent over. . . . And so I think we have to teach students how to live with uncertainty. (Kelly, 1958: 9; italics mine)

He returns to his own experience with his student discussion groups about his manuscript to illustrate how there can be a 'new authority relationship' with students. This is about 'taking people who come as students and changing them into colleagues'. You basically destroy yourself as an authority by saying there are things you, the teacher, do not understand and you involve them in your own perplexities and concerns.

> I think also we need to teach students not to teach. . . . We need to invite students to share in our own efforts if we are trying to solve a problem, if we are doing a piece of research, if we are preparing a manuscript. I think it is very helpful to ask students to help work out the ideas; but I warn you it is also very painful. (Kelly, 1958: 12)

He can be seen as striving to demonstrate his philosophy of *constructive alternativism* at work. There *are* always alternative ways of looking at anything. It seems he actually was abiding by his belief in people conducting their own experiments, of being able to choose from several courses of action and so forth. His main way of doing this was to challenge. One point does come over strongly from the many accounts of student/Kelly interactions, and that is those who answered challenge with challenge seemed to have much less trouble in relating to him than those who did not. Apart from that, it is just possible that Kelly, himself the rebel, actually enjoyed and even encouraged rebellion in others and was therefore disappointed when he did not get it.

Social Relationships and Personal Involvement

Personal construct theory espouses the idea of the 'whole' person; no dichotomy between emotion/feeling and cognition/thinking. But there is no reason why all aspects of our 'being' should run equally smoothly. There is evidence that George Kelly had some problems when it came to inter-personal relationships that involved some element of the personal or the sentimental or the emotional. The question now becomes 'Did George Kelly care?' There are plenty of examples that he did indeed care and care deeply but could not or would not but certainly did not show it. This included being able to say something good about a person. Rue Cromwell says, 'In my experience Kelly was never comfortable offering personal heartfelt support to people face to face.' He gives the story of the differences between Rotter and Kelly in supporting him after he failed an examination.

> Julian Rotter spotted me while peeking through a door window, summoned me by hand wave out into the hallway and, with a warm smile, said 'Ya still have our confidence' and rushed off to some chore. Kelly's expression of support was much longer and highly awkward. He stumbled around as a high school boy with a poorly prepared speech. As I sat through these few minutes in his office, I strangely felt sorrier for him than for me. His sincerity was without doubt, but he was out of his

> role doing this sort of thing. His awkwardness and discomfort left me feeling my failure was magnified rather than reduced. In retrospect I have felt that an element of caring and empathy was what made this difficult for him.

Nowhere is his problem of showing that he cared for others more poignant than in his essay 'Confusion and the clock', written soon after his heart attack. He talks about his feelings for his wife and children. He was referring to this essay when he told me that one of his chapters for his book on 'The Human Feeling' (not completed, but many chapters to be found in Maher, 1969) 'is more autobiographical than I intended'.

> I remember looking up at my wife and thinking of the chilling shock she must be experiencing at that moment. Yet there was no outward sign, only an alertness and a quick efficiency, as she turned here and there to do the things that had to be done. It crossed my mind that I was very proud of her, that she was probably stronger than I was accustomed to give her credit for being, and that there are great resources in the human personality which one can easily overlook in the day-by-day casual living. . . . (Kelly, 1978: 221)
>
> How does this business of human relationships work out? With one person you share too little, and when you go you leave in his memory only the shreds of the legacy he might have had; with another, you share too much, and when you go you leave in his memory altogether too great an emptiness. . . . (Kelly, 1978: 227)
>
> But, it was still Friday morning. I remember the faces of our daughter and son. There was deep concern there, but not, as far as I could see, any sign of panic . . .
>
> There were a thousand and one thoughts, intangible, important, that I had long imagined myself sharing with them, but always these had seemed to require a more propitious moment. So, not only was I lying there in a most unfatherly exhibition of helplessness that must give them none of the sense of security that children have a right to expect of a father in times of emergency, not only was I at the point of leaving them without having properly planned for their future, but I was about to be cut off from the last hope of ever saying to them what was always in my heart. I felt all this, not in sentences, as it is written down here, but altogether in one choking lump . . .
>
> It occurred to me, too, how families always feel guilty when one of them dies, and everyone is inwardly depressed because he remembers how badly he treated the deceased. I know how terrible the pain of this kind of guilt can be, and how much one appreciates some sort of timely reassurance. So, I wanted to reassure the three members of my family standing there – to tell them how perfectly wonderful they had been. But how could I say that, without dramatizing a 'death-bed' scene! So I thought the better of it and kept my mouth shut. (Kelly, 1978: 226)

It was, again, not propitious.

Another example of his not wishing to express his feelings openly was my meeting with him after our correspondence had stretched through the death of my father. I was invited to stay with him and Gladys at the end of a lecture tour across the States from San Francisco to New York. I could not see him as I walked through the airport at Boston so I stopped at the exit and looked around. There he was, silhouetted against a window – just looking and smiling. He hurried over – now that *I* had found *him*, he put his face quite close to mine. 'That's better' he said. The death of my father was never discussed. But I knew he cared.

His caring for others took place in private as many examples of his 'behind the scenes activity' show. Franz Epting says:

> Some time after Kelly died one of the Faculty members in Clinical Psychology at Ohio State asked me if I knew about a telephone call concerning me. It seems that Kelly called this faculty member and asked if certain students had found good positions. Kelly wanted to be helpful in finding these students suitable positions. I was one of the students he asked about and the Faculty member said that yes I had accepted a position at the University of Florida. I was very surprised and of course very very pleased. I had no way of knowing that he would be that mindful of me. Really often not knowing exactly where you stood with Kelly was a problem.

The following comes from Brendan Maher:

> He was a generous man. My wife and I met as graduate students at Ohio State. We both applied for clinical internships at University Medical School. It was a very desirable internship, and the competition was quite keen. We were delighted when both of our applications were approved. We married a few days before the internship began, and only much later learned that George had quietly suggested to the clinical director that we be admitted together wishing to make matters easier for us. He had not asked us, and never mentioned it – our discovery of his benevolence coming much later from another source. . . . George was likely to try to help others quietly. He knew a great deal about the problems and resources of his students, rarely if ever mentioned them but was generous in trying to arrange matters so as to ease the strains of student life. His former secretary had commented more than once on Kelly's many secret kindnesses to students, and how little the students and others were aware of this.

Kelly Through the Eyes of his Own Theory

I do not think that I have 'found' George Kelly, but I feel nearer to him than I did at the start of writing this chapter. In order to summarize the complexities of what I think I know and have found out about George Kelly, I am going to put him under the spotlight of his own theory. I am going to look at him through the eyes of his own 'professional constructs'. These are the constructs he suggests we might find useful in understanding ourselves and others and which, in turn, may suggest a way forward.

In order to listen fully to our client, we must set aside our own construing, particularly those personal values we hold so important. We then listen 'credulously' to get a vague feel for and picture of the world in which the client lives. The personal construct psychotherapist makes no value judgements about what the client says or does.

The Client's Story

I have a picture of a very gifted child growing up on a farm in the Midwest of the United States of America in what years later became known as the great 'dust bowl' of America. His world was one in which there seem to have been very few other children or even other adults besides his parents. Did he learn what it was to be lonely at a very early age? He must certainly have learned to be self-sufficient.

His education up to the age of thirteen seems to have been largely provided by his mother and his father, a Presbyterian minister before he became a farmer. He no doubt worked on the farm as we know that he milked the cows at dawn.

There were two influences which may have led to his ability to burst through the boundaries of his own thoughts. There was his isolated life on the Kansas plain and there were the stories of his maternal grandfather, captain of a ship sailing the North Atlantic. Both are concerned with life bounded only by the horizon and both are about self-sufficiency. Perhaps 'the truth', life, knowledge, were always over that horizon?

It seems that his first experience of any prolonged formal education was at the age of thirteen when he went to live away from home to attend the high school at Wichita. He attended four different schools in the next four years. We have no information about why this was. There can be little doubt that George Kelly missed out on what would normally be seen as the socialization process.

We can ask ourselves two questions here. What did George Kelly think of himself as he left home and joined others of his age? And what did other children think of George Kelly, aged thirteen? There is virtually no information available to me to answer either of these questions, but some answers to the second question can be guessed at.

With a history of lack of peers and other adults for the usual socialization process to take place, we must hypothesize that, when he did go to school at the age of thirteen, he would experience difficulties. The psychological literature is surprisingly sparse when it comes to such early social deprivation. But it is known that children do not take readily to the 'unusual' nor to non-conformists. George Kelly would no doubt be a child who did not seem to know about the 'rules' of interacting with other children; who was poor; who no doubt knew a great deal more than they did; and who may well have quickly withdrawn into himself; perhaps he became ever more self-sufficient and rebellious? He may have experienced boredom, being a gifted child, well in advance educationally and intellectually of his peers. Was his behaviour disruptive? There must have been some reason for his change of schools four times in the next four years.

His subsequent history shows a further pattern of changing schools and colleges and subjects: a pattern which gave him considerable pleasure to recount. We also know that he found he had acting skills.

His first period of stability would seem to have been at Fort Hays Kansas State College. His years there gave him the chance to use his creative skills in developing new ways of providing psychological services to schools spread over the vast plains of Kansas, and ways of helping children with problems.

His five years in the services again gave him opportunities to be creative and develop new approaches to existing problems. But perhaps he also, for the first time, found out what it was like to live within a rigid system. Here there would be discipline and rules not to mention a commitment to a cause. There is an underlying theme of discipline running through the years together with a sense of the importance of each person committing themselves to whatever they take on.

Kelly now committed himself to clinical psychology in a very profound way, playing a major role in the development of the discipline. It is said that he believed the profession of clinical psychology was more important than the individual students who were studying it, which may or may not be true. He certainly seemed to want his students to be the best because in that way clinical psychology could hold its head up high. Perhaps he also wanted them to be the best to prove to others (and to himself?) that he was a person of account?

A Transitive Diagnosis

So much for a brief history of George Kelly. What about a transitive diagnosis? One of Kelly's own methods with his clinical students was to present them with a figure of, say, Saint Paul, and ask them to work out a 'transitive diagnosis'. In personal construct psychotherapy the diagnosis is the planning stage of treatment. Without a diagnosis, no therapist can start helping a client – it is the diagnosis that guides the therapy.

There are two main aspects of a personal construct transitive diagnosis. One is concerned with process and conceptual structure, and the other with content. It is usually not possible to disentangle them completely.

Process and Structure In terms of process, we have a picture of a man who could swing from extremely *tight* construing to something that is quite *loose*. That is, he was a man who kept himself and his students under tight control. There were rules of dress and behaviour that were rigidly adhered to. But, when something caught his imagination, he could suddenly change to that mode of thinking that allows for 'playing with ideas'. In his theory he made both these modes of thought form the lynch-pin of the *creativity* cycle. You cannot be creative unless you are able to loosen your thinking and so come up with an idea that is novel, and you cannot make use of that new idea unless you tighten up on it so as to look it in the face. If such sudden shifts take place in public, the person can be very confusing to others.

The structure of George Kelly's construing system was obviously complex. The best professional construct I can invoke here is *fragmentation*. As this corollary says: *A person may successively employ a variety of construction subsystems which are inferentially incompatible with each other*. For instance, the loving father who beats the living daylights out of his son because 'you spare the rod and spoil the child'. Fragmentation can appear inconsistent or irrational but as Kelly comments:

> Perhaps I should add that I do not see this kind of 'irrationality' as necessarily a bad thing. For man logic and inference can be as much an obstacle to his ontological ventures as a guide to them. (Kelly, 1970a: 20)

I see at least two inferentially incompatible subsystems within George Kelly's construing. There is the man of vision, the thinker of great thoughts, the writer, the possible world-changer; the man who enjoyed humour and wit, even sometimes at the expense of others; the man who sought challenge. This was clearly his preferred world; the world of looser construing; the world of the horizons which can be transcended if only we try hard enough. Here lives George Kelly the iconoclast.

The other subsystem is to do with 'getting the job done' in a world of others. He seems to have found it necessary to live some parts of his life in a rule-bound world. The rules and the 'roles' he adopted enabled him to carry out many functions to which he had committed himself without becoming 'personally' involved. Such construing can cause problems for the person when their tight construing is invalidated – something happens that does not conform to the rules.

If the invoking of the idea of fragmentation is anywhere near a reasonable hypothesis, then my guess is that George Kelly was perceived as such a complex man because he had more than just two such construing subsystems.

Threat and Guilt How do people sustain themselves with fragmented construing systems? They may have one or more overarching, superordinate, possibly core role constructs. One such may have been something to do with his religious beliefs, while another may have been to do with the sort of person he saw himself as being, in terms of his background of poverty and lack of education relative to his current academic status and success. Al Landfield tells of one of the very few personal comments George Kelly is known to have made. That is his saying to Al Landfield, 'I live my life under constant threat.' Threat is the awareness of an imminent comprehensive need for core role reconstruing.

This threat might have been to do with his religion. He was a self-confessed practising Christian when it was not a particularly popular thing to be. Yet he viewed both religion and science as creative processes. He used religious examples in his writings that must have made some orthodox Christians squirm. Did he even lose his faith? For instance, what did he mean by: 'And our theologies, far-seeing as they appear to be, do, in time, lead to such indecent practices that sensitive men refuse any longer to take them literally. Thus we find ourselves repeatedly cut off from what once we thought we knew for sure, and we must reluctantly abandon the very faiths from which we originally launched our most fruitful enterprises' (Kelly, 1977: 5)? Or, did he, on occasion, stretch his mind to the limits and see personal construct theory as a way of extending Christianity? Or was he re-writing the scriptures? If these were possibilities, what an enormous sense of threat that must have produced in him in the cold light of the present.

Another very possible threat is to be found in his childhood. Did he continue to construe himself as 'poor and an outsider'? In terms of his own theory, did he 'fail to up-date his construing'? Was his perceived need for tight control over himself and his students and colleagues partly concerned with the need to keep his early life known only to himself? He knew it was there. Could it be that being a successful person was at odds with his core role that he was really only an impoverished farmer's son from Kansas? This would mean he was playing a lie. That could be threat coupled with guilt (awareness of dislodgement from one's core role). He would be threatened more and more as the evidence of his success accrued, and experience guilt whenever he came to 'believe' he actually was a world-renowned psychologist.

Sociality is another aspect of personal construct theory that one might usefully invoke here, with its re-definition of 'role' as follows: *to the extent that one person construes the construction processes of another, he may play a role in a social process involving the other person.*

There has been considerable discussion about the extent to which Kelly construed the construction processes of those students who saw his behaviour as destructive. We know that he was aware of the destructive effect he sometimes had on them. His own writings say that we may *attempt* to play a 'role' in relation to others, but

> my construing of your construction processes need not be accurate in order for me to play a role in a social process that involves you. I have seen a person play a role, and do it most effectively – even in a manner quite acceptable to his colleagues – when he grossly misperceived their outlooks, and they knew it. But because he did what he did on the basis of what he thought they understood, not merely on the basis of their overt acts, he was able to play a collaborative role in a social process whose experiential cycle led them all somewhere. (Kelly, 1970a: 24)

So playing a social role in relation to others does not mean that you necessarily get it right. There is much evidence that Kelly did acknowledge that he sometimes got things wrong and took radical steps to change when he was challenged. We do know that his behaviour to his students was designed to be a deliberate challenge. Was he, in fact, inaccurate in his construing of his students' construing of him, or was he so committed to his belief in 'teaching by challenging' that he did not stop until *they* challenged *him*? These are all obviously in the realms of speculation, but illustrate the sort of thinking the formulation of a transitive diagnosis leads one to do.

A Suitable Case for Treatment?

Having attempted a transitive diagnosis as a way of summarizing what I have gleaned about George Kelly, the man, I can ask whether he might have benefited from psychotherapy. My personal answer is 'no'. He did not seek it. Did he have what might be called 'a problem'? My answer is 'yes'. For example, maybe he could have been helped to deal with whatever it was that he said threatened him. But he chose not to. He was a great man who thought great thoughts and produced great works *because he was the man he was*. Let George Kelly have the last word:

> Often it is the uninferred fragment of a man's construction system that makes him great, whereas if he were an integrated whole – taking into account all that the whole would have to embrace – the poor fellow would be no better than his 'natural self'. (Kelly, 1970a: 20)

Has anybody here seen Kelly?
Find him if you can!

Notes

1 All the quotations in this chapter for which I give no specific source come from these personal communications, 1994–5.

2 All Kelly quotations in this chapter which are given no specific source come from this autobiography, found among the papers kept by Gladys Kelly.

2

Major Contributions to Theory

THE THEORY OF PSYCHOTHERAPY

In 1955 George Kelly presented us with a theory about how we try to make sense of the world and events that constantly bombard us. The person who wants help in this task is seen as no different from anyone else. That person is just finding it more difficult to make sense of events and the world. Sometimes we develop a 'symptom'. This is one way of 'making sense of otherwise chaotic experiences'.

One essential feature of Kelly's work is that personal construct psychotherapy stems directly from personal construct theory. Another way of putting it is to say that personal construct psychotherapy is one example of personal construct theory in action.

Before moving on, it is important to indicate the difference between a concept and a construct. One of the influences on Kelly's thinking can be seen in his unpublished book 'Understandable Psychology' (1932). Kelly cites Johann Herbart as being the first to attempt to apply psychology to the problems of teaching and, in so doing, makes the distinction between concepts and constructs.

> Johann Friedrich Herbart (1776–1841) was both a philosopher and a scientific pedagogue. . . . According to his doctrine of the *apperceptive mass* the mind could not accept a new idea unless it fitted into the ideas which were conscious at the time. In trying to recall or set up an idea the apperceptive mass, or background of previous experience, must always be taken into consideration. Our perceptions are then really more than perceptions, they are apperceptions, experiences into which all past experiences are fused as well as the object of the moment. (Kelly, 1932: 218)

A 'construct' is more than a 'concept' in several ways. As suggested by Herbart, a construct is embedded in a 'system' of constructs. Constructs have been developed over the years, been modified as they are used, and sometimes found wanting. Constructs are also bi-polar. They indicate what aspects of a situation are similar to *and thereby* different from other aspects of that situation – a plate is like other plates in certain respects and thereby is different from saucers. A concept deals only with similarities – a plate is a plate and is different from all other items in our world. Most importantly, constructs form the basis for prediction. This is fundamental to the personal construct notion that the person is a process. A fuller comparison between concepts and constructs can be found in Fransella, 1989.

One way of looking at Kelly's contributions to the theory and practice of psychotherapy is to see how personal construct theory differs from other theories that were around in 1955. Essentially, the two main theoretical approaches were psychodynamic, stemming largely from the ideas of Sigmund Freud and resulting in various forms of psychoanalysis, and the behavioural. The behavioural model was of two main types. There was the classical conditioning model coming from Ivan Pavlov and the operant conditioning model coming from B. F. Skinner.

In this intellectual context personal construct theory was very radical. In some ways it is still radical in the mid-1990s. Kelly's influence on the 'cognitive revolution' which ousted behaviourism from its place in mainstream psychology should not be underestimated. At the 1995 International Congress on Personal Construct Psychology in Barcelona, the eminent psychologist Jerome Bruner said 'Kelly was the knight in the dust-bowl of the Mid West who set out to slay the dragon of S–R psychology – and he won!'.

Personal Construct Theory Has a Philosophy

It may not seem unusual for a psychological theory to have a stated philosophy. But it was in 1955 and it is now. All theories of the person, of course, have a philosophy about the sort of person they are describing. But their philosophy is usually implicit or deeply buried. Since psychology as a discipline arose from the soil of philosophy, and much of early psychology involved a battle to show just how very different it was, it did not take kindly to Kelly's insistence that philosophy should be part of its subject matter – certainly not four decades ago.

But Kelly showed that after the antithesis between philosophy and psychology could come the synthesis. He based his whole psychology of personal constructs upon a philosophy of his own that he called *constructive alternativism.* Its essential statement is:

> *We assume that all of our present interpretations of the universe are subject to revision or replacement.* . . . . . . there are always some alternative constructions available to choose among in dealing with the world. No one needs to paint himself into a corner, no one needs to be

> completely hemmed in by circumstances; no one needs to be the victim of his biography. (Kelly, 1991, Vol. 1: 11)

Kelly later extended that last statement to say that we can indeed become a victim of our biography if we construe it that way. He loved to play the American science game of inventing new, complex words. But when it can be seen how constructive alternativism relates to *alternative constructions*, it becomes obvious.

This is not a home-spun, idiosyncratic philosophy that cobbles together existing ideas. It is one which shows him to have been 'philosophically literate' (Warren, 1989: 298). This is supported by a chapter in Kelly's unpublished book 'Understandable Psychology' (1932) entitled 'The history and the systems of psychology', in which he traces philosophy as it applies to psychology through from Aristotle to 1932.

Kelly's philosophy has two basic but related aspects. One is to do with the nature of truth and knowledge and the other is to do with the nature of reality. These obviously overlap.

The Nature of Truth and Knowledge

Kelly entered a philosophical minefield here. This has to do with the controversial fields of epistemology and metaphysics which ask interconnected questions about 'how we might know reality' and 'the ultimate nature of reality'. In Bill Warren's view, Kelly seems to be experiencing the same difficulty that philosophers experience, that of sliding between the two fields when he talks of 'truth'. What Kelly seems to have tried to do is to have made the idea of truth a link between these two controversial fields of philosophical endeavour. This is an example of Kelly not being a man who shied away from the controversial.

It is important to note that Kelly is not saying that there is 'no true reality out there'. He was at pains to say he was *not* an 'idealist'. He makes clear from the outset 'that it is a real world we shall be talking about, not a world composed solely of the flitting shadows of people's thoughts' (Kelly, 1991, Vol. 1: 5). So, *no one has direct access to the truth*. Each person reading that statement will have his or her own unique understanding of it. As the Individuality Corollary of the theory states, we all construe the world of events differently. We do, naturally, share some common ground (Commonality Corollary), otherwise we could not communicate at all. But that common ground will never be one hundred per cent. People participating in the same event will all see it differently – if for no other reason than that each has a different 'self' on the centre of that stage. Whose stage is the 'true' one?

In saying that no one of us can say that 'my perception of this event is the *true* one and yours is false' Kelly is following the thinking of the philosopher Kant. It is interesting to note that in 'Understandable Psychology' (1932) Kelly makes only one reference to Kant's philosophy:

> Immanuel Kant (1724–1804), the great German philosopher, discarded Leibnitz's theory of monads and concentrated his attention on the nature of mind before experience touches it. This lack of interest in the part which experience plays tended to divorce his philosophy from the psychological train. (Kelly, 1932: 218)

Kelly also mentions Vaihinger and his 'as if' philosophy (1924) as having influenced his ideas.

> In it he offered a system of thought in which God and reality might best be represented as paradigms. This was not to say that either God or reality was any less certain than anything else in the realm of man's awareness, but only that all matters confronting man might best be regarded in hypothetical ways. (Kelly, 1969c: 149)

Kelly points out that Alfred Adler was also influenced by Vaihinger's philosophy. Adler agreed with Vaihinger that individuals often behave 'as if' circumstances were absolutely true, for instance that 'life is dangerous', or 'I am weak', or 'people cannot be trusted'. People have problems when these 'fictive notions' are challenged. Kelly quotes Adler as saying:

> I, myself, as the inventor of the 'inferiority complex', have never thought of it as of a spirit, knowing that it has never been in the consciousness or unconsciousness of the patient but only in my own consciousness, and have used it rather for illumination so that the patient could see his attitude in the right coherence. (Adler, 1937: 774)

In his paper 'The language of hypothesis' (1969c), Kelly suggests that one of our problems in giving up the idea of a 'true' reality is that we use the indicative mood in our language. The various forms of the verb *to be* in the indicative mood allow us to say 'that is a fact of life', or 'he is suffering from schizophrenia'. That makes us attribute the condition to the object rather than to our interpretation of that object. He suggests that a change to the use of the *invitational mood* in our language would make it easier for us to accept that 'truth' is beyond our grasp. Kelly states it thus:

> Suppose our verbs could be cast in the *invitational mood*. This is to say that instead of being used in the popular *indicative mood* of objective speech . . . a verb could be cast in a form which would suggest to the listener that a certain novel interpretation of an object might be entertained. For example, I might say, 'Suppose we regard the floor as if it were hard.'

> If I make such a statement I immediately find myself in an interesting position. The statement leaves both the speaker and the listener, not with a conclusion on their hands, but in a posture of expectancy – suppose we do regard the floor as if it were hard, what then? A verb employed in the invitational mood . . . would have the effect of orienting one to the future, not merely to the present or to the past. It would set the stage for prediction of what is to ensue. It suggests that the floor is open to a variety of interpretations or constructions. It invites the listener to cope with his circumstances – in this case, the floor – in new ways. But more than this, it suggests that the view of the floor as something hard is one that is not imposed upon us from without, nor is it isolated from external evidence, as a phenomenological proposition would be, but is one that can be pursued, tested, abandoned, or reconsidered at a later time. (Kelly, 1969c: 149)

One other result of such a change in language would be that we have to take responsibility for our statements.

The problem of the use of the verb *to be* has been commented on by philosophers for many years. It was taken up by the founder of general semantics, Korzybski (1933). Kelly cites Korzybski as one of the people who had also influenced his thinking. He says in his 'The autobiography of a theory':

> Korzbyski's newly published *Science and Sanity* raised questions about the ways in which language and thought are interrelated. . . .
>
> Not only did it seem that the words man uses give and hold the structure of his thought, but, more particularly, the names by which he calls himself give and hold the structure of his personality. Each of us invests his name with a particular kind of meaning. It has been so for thousands of years. The man who knew himself as 'Saul' became the man who martyred himself as 'Paul', perhaps in a way that would have been impossible if he had persisted in identifying himself as 'Saul'. (Kelly, 1969a: 56)

McWilliams (1993) ties this all together with the approach from general semantics called E-prime (Bourland and Johnston, 1991). Basically, E-prime makes the person take responsibility for a statement – as does the invitational mood. Thus, 'he is an idiot' does not make the statement 'true' although the language appears to. If we change that statement to become 'he looks like an idiot' or 'he behaves like an idiot' we have implicitly added the words 'to me'. McWilliams points out that Albert Ellis realized the power of E-prime to draw the client's attention to personally damaging statements. Ellis used E-prime in the revised editions of several of his rational–emotive psychotherapy books (for example, Ellis, 1975; 1976; 1977).

The Nature of Reality

The nature of construing, for Kelly, is that we place our own constructions upon the reality that we perceive. In that sense, our reality is created by ourselves – it is of our own making.

Living involves the person representing to themselves the environment in which he or she lives. Because we can represent the world to ourselves, we can place alternative constructions upon it. We can change the environment or our constructions of it when it does not come up to our expectations.

> . . . our formulation . . . emphasizes the creative capacity of the living thing to represent the environment, not merely to respond to it. Because he can represent his environment, he can place alternative constructions upon it and, indeed, do something about it if it doesn't suit him. To the living creature, then, the universe is real, but it is not inexorable unless he chooses to construe it that way. (Kelly, 1991, Vol. 1: 6)

It may seem as if we can misrepresent events to ourselves. But that is a misstatement. The misrepresentations are only so in the eye of the onlooker – to the beholder they are real. Delusions or hallucinations are real or true to the person experiencing them. *To understand another we have to put on their spectacles and see how they represent the world to themselves.*

A major debate about the nature of reality concerns whether it is 'real' (realism) or 'in the mind' (idealism). The *realism* of behaviourists was not for Kelly nor, in fact was its opposite pole – *idealism*. Rychlak (1968) says of Kelly:

> Though he does not like to be identified as blatantly idealistic, we do Kelly no injustice in placing his theory closer to this pole than to the pole of realism. In fact, Kelly has already named the opposite pole of the dimension on which he rests . . . he explicitly stated: 'But I am not a realist – not anymore – and I do not believe either the client or the therapist has to lie down and let facts crawl over him'. (Kelly, 1969d: 227; Rychlak, 1968: 21)

Some time between 1929 and 1945 Kelly wrote a poem (now among his unpublished papers) which seems to me to be on this subject.

ONTA

1

(Parmenides) Is so!

The men who grasp and clutch at objects say,
'Now look; this is reality.

It's firm. It's bold and clear.
So straight would be tomorrow's flimsy way
If you would only deign to see
Just that that's here, that's here.'

To this what shall I say?

One cannot but agree.

I too am surely here.

2

(Alexander) But why for man?

The men who talk and talk in order to be wise
Yap loud and long at shadows in our night
And snarl at strangers constantly.
Alone, they strive their dreams to guard with peering eyes
Till dawn, or death – or both – shall prove them right
And what is not at last shall be.

But who utters truth until he tries?

To save their dreams all men must fight.

My world shall take its shape from me!

3

(Paul) Man lives. Man dies. What then?

The men who climb the distant heights to gain some crystal tower,
From thence to visualize the space beyond their time.
Chart past and future as one coursing stream,
Find themselves, borne in its flow, transcending troubled hours.
So thus, in lives with greater destinies aligned,
Self's immortality is seen.

And I? Why dare not I attune to greater power?

Indeed, all's lost, astray from its majestic line.

I'll dangle neither truth nor gods upon a string!

4

(Xenos) Once this I knew and had forgot

The men who lived to live, whose names are lost among discarded years,
No pedant questions posed. Their words stood not for things apart
But only served to draw them close to what was theirs.
Self was for them a woman's voice, a tiny hand, a storm, a tear,
A sorrow etched in love. They left no legacy of art,
Yet overhead we hear their children climbing up the stairs.

To whom but them has what is real approached so near?
This is no alien world; its keys are in my heart.
I touch, I try, I scan, I feel, and stumble up my stairs.

An important aspect of construing is abstraction. Kelly tells of Korzybski's influence again here. Korzybski said we create our reality by selecting material from the flow of life around us by abstracting it. In this sense our mental representations or abstractions of the world are not identical to 'how it really is'. We then create words to label these abstractions.

Stewart and Barry (1991) say that Korzybski leaned heavily on the ideas of the physicist Ernst Mach (1838–1916). We can speculate that perhaps Kelly had come across Mach's ideas while he was studying physics. Perhaps these ideas caught his fancy and he did not know, at that time, what to do with them.

Kelly was learning physics when Einstein's ideas and those of quantum mechanics were challenging the Newtonian view of science. So it is interesting to compare one of Kelly's philosophical statements about the nature of reality with those of Albert Einstein, who says:

> Physical concepts are free creations of the human mind, and are not, however it may seem, uniquely determined by the external world. In our endeavor to understand reality we are somewhat like a man trying to understand the mechanism of a closed watch. He sees the face and the moving hands, even hears its ticking, but he has no way of opening the case. If he is ingenious he may form some picture of a mechanism which could be responsible for all the things he observes, but he may never be quite sure his picture is the only one which could explain his observations. He will never be able to compare his picture with the real mechanism and he cannot even imagine the possibility or the meaning of such a comparison. (Einstein and Infeld, 1938: 31)

Some decades later Kelly was saying:

> The fact that my only approach to reality is through offering some responsible construction of it does not discourage me from postulating that it is there. The open question for man is not whether reality exists or not, but what he can make of it. (Kelly, 1969e: 25)

How reality is construed has implications for how science is construed and, in Kelly's framework, how the client is construed.

The realism expressed by Isaac Newton and the behaviourists saw science as exploring the real world which can, potentially at least, be mapped. The role of science from the realist's point of view is to find out 'the facts' about the world. That is done by conducting experiments.

For this Newtonian, realist view of science, Kelly coined another tongue-in-cheek term *accumulative fragmentalism*. The Newtonian scientist regards the world as real and seeks to verify a hypothesis – determine whether it is *really* true. Kelly says:

> To the accumulative fragmentalist the next step is to find another nugget of truth . . . the only grounds for entertaining further questions about the matter is evidence that he was wrong. Since this kind of nuisance may pop up at any time he is careful to replicate his experiments and make sure the answer to his question is absolutely, positively, and irrevocably right! (Kelly, 1969f: 126)

The modern theoretical physicist David Bohm makes the point that there is nothing intrinsically wrong in dividing aspects of our world into manageable chunks, but that it does us a disservice when we apply such strategies to ourselves.

> Being guided by a fragmentary self-world view, man then acts in such a way as to try to break himself and the world up, so that all seems to correspond to his way of thinking. Man thus obtains apparent proof of the correctness of his fragmentary self-world view though, of course, he overlooks the fact that it is he himself, acting according to his mode of thought, who has brought about the fragmentation that now seems to have an autonomous existence, independent of his will and of his desire. (Bohm, 1980: 2–3)

The idealists, on the other hand, would not concern themselves with science and experiments at all. Kelly has taken the unusual and middle position stating both that there is a reality but that we only have access to the reality we have created. In the case of his own model of science based on *constructive alternativism*, the scientist is seen as seeking to confirm predictions:

> To the constructive alternativist the next step is to see if he can improve his hypothesis, perhaps by formulating his questions in new ways or by pursuing the implications of some fresh assumption that occurred to him when he was writing up the conclusions to his last experiment. (Kelly, 1969f: 127)

The direct relevance of all this to psychotherapy is put by Kelly as follows:

> While I have been talking about scientists everything I have been saying applies equally to persons who do not claim to be scientists. A psychotherapy patient who accumulates things in pieces such as 'good habits', 'clever solutions', 'sound knowledge' and tokens of 'meritorious achievements' is likely to let his life get into pretty bad shape before he starts letting go of what he has acquired. And when he does start to let go everything seems to crumble at once. He had assumed that once his

> conclusions were verified there would be no point in exploring further what had already been demonstrated to be true. To make matters worse, every proposition his therapist offers or encourages becomes a threat, for it implies a sweeping invalidation of his way of life and a further spread of chaos that has already engulfed him. The therapist will find himself called upon to exercise great skill in helping such a person collect his wits enough to venture anything new. (Kelly 1969f: 127)

The client who is already a constructive alternativist in outlook, or who has become one during the course of therapy, is not threatened in this way with the prospect of change. He or she has seen that they do not have to give up one hypothesis before contemplating another. They are able and willing to experiment with life. This is a vital aspect of Kelly's philosophy and plays a central role in personal construct psychotherapy.

Anyone wanting to train in the personal construct approach to therapy and counselling has to start from this philosophical standpoint.

Kelly's Philosophy and Theory in Context

It is clear that Kelly was philosophically literate, and it is possible to use his own writings to help place his own constructive alternativism and theory in the context of other philosophies. Personal construct theory is most commonly described as being a phenomenological theory. Kelly talks of phenomenology as early as 1932 in the last chapter of his unpublished book, 'The history and the systems of psychology'.

> Brentano tremendously influenced Carl Stumpf (1848–) who is next in the line of act psychologists. Stumpf's principal interest was in music, but he combined his interest and his academic vocation. He became a philosopher, for in Germany psychology has always been considered a branch of philosophy, and made his principal contributions in the field of the psychology of music. . . . Stumpf carried forward the Brentano tradition of *act* psychology, but one of his students, Husserl (1859–1938) altered the doctrine slightly. He distinguished between the acts and the phenomena. There grew up around this distinction a system of psychology called *phenomenology*. In the pure act psychology it was the act of the organism that was the subject of psychology; in phenomenology it was the event toward which the act was directed. (Kelly, 1932: 220–3)

Then, in 1959 Kelly was talking again about his theory:

> Is it a phenomenological theory? Granted that . . . phenomenology comes in various shapes and sizes, our (fundamental) postulate does not make the usual phenomenological commitments. We did not say, for example, that one is surrounded only by his perceptions. In fact, we started this discussion by asserting that there is a sense in which all of us

> are caught up in our circumstances. Nor do we say that each personal world is an island universe. The words 'personal' and 'private' are certainly not synonyms. I think the tree that falls in the primeval forest makes a bang just like any other tree. Moreover, we might sometime, although at the moment I cannot say how, take an interest in the noise that centuries ago nobody heard and eventually make something scientifically important out of it. (Kelly, 1959a: 6)

Warren (1989) has analysed constructive alternativism in the context of philosophy generally. He points out that Husserl's later ideas, combined with those of Heidegger, lead to existential phenomenology, which concerned itself with the particularly human aspects of phenomena, captured in the term *Lebenswelt* or 'life world'. Warren feels that Kelly would have felt much more in tune with this later development with its efforts to understand individual and group 'life worlds'. Warren concludes that as philosophy becomes more concerned with process and change, 'personal construct theory comes more and more into prominence and its philosophical integrity becomes more obvious' (Warren, 1989: 287).

The place of constructive alternativism in relation to 'constructivism', which assumed prominence in the 1980s, is discussed in Chapter 4.

Personal Construct Theory Sees the Person as a Whole

If we look at the major trends of psychology this century, we find that people have focused on different aspects of the person. Those following the psychodynamic approach to human understanding pay most attention to human emotions and motivation but say little about thought processes. Those using the behavioural approach focus, obviously, on behaviour and, quite often, on motivation in terms of needs and drives, but have little to say about emotion except in so far as it relates to behaviour.

One of Kelly's most important contributions to our attempts to understand ourself and others is his rejection of the body–mind dichotomy. For him, thinking and feeling are indivisible.

Kelly tried to encompass all aspects of human experiencing within his single theory of personal constructs. We are forms of motion. We are experiencing, living beings. We are our feelings, our thoughts, our 'unconscious processes'. He tried to build into his theory descriptions of everything we talk about as relating to being human – learning, motivation, emotions, perceptions. His very strong feeling that the division of mind and body had done us all a disservice was by no means the generally accepted view. People who argue that personal construct therapy is a cognitive therapy (see

Chapter 4) fail to grasp that Kelly formulated a theory about human experiencing. This means it is essentially a theory about change, about process. Construing is not 'thinking' *or* 'feeling' – it is the act of discriminating experientially. It is the way in which we have perceived – at some level of awareness – that certain events around us are repeating themselves and are thereby different from other events. Once we have noted similarities and differences (discriminated) between events, we can anticipate future events.

Experiencing and construing are part and parcel of the same process. We can no more construe without experiencing than we can experience without construing.

> The classic distinction that separates these two constructs (emotion, cognition) has, in the manner of most classic distinctions that once were useful, become a barrier to sensitive psychological inquiry. When one so divides the experience of man it becomes difficult to make the most of the holistic aspirations that may infuse the science of psychology with new life. (Kelly, 1969g: 140)

Kelly integrates emotional experiences within his theory by relating them to an awareness that our construing system is in a state of transition or is inadequate for construing the events which confront us. We *experience* the transition or inadequacy, we do not *think* it.

It is important to distinguish here between personal construct *theory* and *personal* construing. Just because the theory says construing is about both thinking and feeling does not mean that we or a client needs to see (construe) it that way. The client may well construe *body* and *mind* as 'interacting'. It makes no sense to us as clinicians to say 'the body and mind interact' but it may make sense to the client, and it is the client's construing we will be trying to understand.

Details of these emotions as defined by Kelly are given in the next section of this chapter.

There are many in psychology who insist that the distinction between body and mind *is a fact* – it is real. Kelly said the distinction is not a fact but just one way of giving meaning to the complexities of the person. Many psychologists do not seem able to think in other than Cartesian dualistic terms. Perhaps we could use personal construct theory and suggest that some of these psychologists are being hostile. That is, they are continuing to extort evidence to support their view that dualism is alive and well while, at some level of awareness, they do know that there are alternative ways of viewing it.

Personal Construct Theory Has an Explicit Model of the Person

Not surprisingly considering his training, Kelly's model of the person is that of the scientist. Anticipation and prediction are central to all science.

Kelly pointed out that psychologists like to think of themselves as scientists. They want to be able to predict and control events. He asked why it was that psychologists denied such rights to the 'subject' of the experiment. What would happen, he asked, if we looked at each one of us 'as if' we were also scientists? – each aiming to predict and control the course of events with which we are involved; each having theories; each testing hypotheses derived from these theories; and each weighing up the experimental evidence.

This model has an implication which Kelly did not elaborate until some time after the publication of his major work in 1955. In the usual psychological experiment, it is behaviour that is the dependent variable. Behaviour is the end result which we are seeking to predict and control. But Kelly changed the nature of the behaviour within the experimental paradigm. Let us say that I have a theory, at some level of awareness, that I have established a good relationship with the client before me. I then hypothesize that if I inquire about his relationship with his father – which I believe to be central to his problem – he will tell me. The only way in which I will know that his relationship with me is as I hypothesize is by my behaving – I ask him. Kelly spelled this out in his paper 'Behaviour is an experiment':

> Take, for example, the reverse snake charming experiment, which has become the popular prototype for behaviour therapy. The task is for a person who shudders at the sight of snakes to come to appreciate how very charming a snake can be. The first step is to entertain the hypothesis . . . The next step is to make a behavioral investment, that is to say, to pose the question behaviorally. (Kelly, 1970b: 268)

What the behaviour therapist does is to establish the boundaries of each experiment so that the scientist (the client) knows whether his experiment has validated his hypothesis or not.

Seeing behaviour as an experiment (a question) rather than an end result (an answer) has a profound effect on the whole of the psychotherapeutic process as well as our attempts to understand others. We do not 'judge' a person on the basis of their behaviour. We do not 'interpret' his or her behaviour on the basis of some personal theory of ours. Instead, we ask a question – just as the client is asking a question by behaving as he or she does. So we ask:

'What experiment is my client conducting that is making her behave in this way?' There is another implication of profound importance. If the client's behaviour is viewed as a way of testing his or her personal theories about how life is, then the psychotherapist's own behaviour *becomes a validator of the client's construing*. How the therapist interacts with the client is crucial to the process.

Personal Construct Theory Treats People as Actors, Not Reactors

One of the aspects of both psychodynamic theory and behaviourist theory that Kelly most disliked was the way in which they treat the person 'as if' each of us is pushed and pulled by events rather than being in charge of ourselves. This does not mean that we can each do exactly what we would like to do. We are constrained by the social and physical contexts in which we live, and by how we represent that situation to ourselves. But we are also able to prise ourselves away from those representations – sometimes it takes the help of a psychotherapist – in order to see if there is not some other way of construing events that would suit us better and thereby give us greater control over those events in the future. We create our own reality; we create ourselves.

Personal Construct Theory Does Away with the Concept of Motivation

Kelly felt no need to copy the physical sciences as other theorists have done by postulating that physical matter is inert and some force has to make it move. The behaviourists cite innate or learned drives or 'needs' to make us do things. Freud derived the concept of 'psychic energy' from the concept of physical energy. The 'unconscious' is seen as being where all psychic energy resides and, from there, it supplies energy to all parts of the personality and thus energizes our psychological processes.

Kelly argued that we do not have to mimic the physical sciences. We are dealing with living rather than inert matter, and one vital aspect of living matter is that it moves. We do not have to explain why it does so, just why it moves in that particular direction.

> Life itself could be defined as a form of process or movement. Thus, designating man as our object of psychological inquiry, we would be taking it for granted that movement was an essential property of his being, not something that had to be accounted for separately. We would be talking about a form of movement – man – not something that had to be motivated. (Kelly, 1969h: 80)

Another reason why he felt it important to eliminate the concept of motivation is that our understanding of someone is not increased when we use our own interpretations of their behaviour and attribute a 'motive' to him or her. We may describe someone as 'lazy' and yet, when we observe what they are actually doing, we find they are being very 'active'. They are just *not* doing what *we* think they *should* be doing.

Kelly built the motivating aspects of the person into his Choice Corollary. *A person chooses for himself that alternative in a dichotomized construct through which he anticipates the greater possibility for extension and definition of his system.*

We each aim to make our world more predictable and thus more personally meaningful. Our choice does not always seem logical to the outsider. The corollary says that we *choose* to be the person we are, however much we may feel we want to change. The client's problem has – in some sense – been *chosen* because it offers greater possibilities for extension and definition of his or her construct system.

We have each made choices between certain courses of action and we are stuck with those choices until we choose to change. It is often the case in personal construct psychotherapy that the first hill to climb is to persuade the client to act 'as if' he or she had made certain choices – no one forced them to be as they are. They have to take some responsibility for the predicament in which they find themselves. At some point in the psychotherapy the client must give up the plea that he is a victim of circumstances or 'it is not my fault'. An example of the use of the Choice Corollary in attempting to get a new slant on a long-term problem can be found in Chapter 5, in the description of my work with those who stutter. It is important to emphasize here that 'making choices' is not equivalent to making *conscious* choices. Much construing goes on at lower levels of cognitive awareness; this will be elaborated on in the second part of this chapter.

This theme of freedom of choice and the individual assuming responsibility for our actions comes very early in Kelly's writings. In 1927 he wrote a document entitled: 'A plan for socializing Friends University with respect to student participation in school control'. In the preface Kelly writes that although his degree was not from Friends, he did spend three of his undergraduate years there and believes 'that the school has contributed more to my education than has any other institution'. He was a member of the Student Council and chairman of a committee for the revision of the Student Government Association Constitution. Chapter 5 of this unpublished document is entitled 'Arousing Discontent: building on problems rather than on organizations'. In it he says:

> The whole system of participation must be built upon problems which actually exist and are felt to exist. The students should be aroused to a point where they will not be content with anything less than a whole-hearted attempt to find solutions. They must assume the responsibility for the solving of problems which the Faculty has hitherto assumed. Because one student takes upon himself a personal concern of the way a class is conducted, is no reason the instructor should feel that the student is intruding. In fact, the method of conducting a class is of more vital importance to the student than to the teacher. It is his education and he is giving valuable time and energy, why shouldn't he be concerned? (Kelly, 1927)

This same theme of encouraging the student to take responsibility for their own life was seen in Chapter 1 in relation to Kelly's own teaching strategies.

McWilliams (1980) has suggested a connection between the motivating aspects of the Choice Corollary and types of scientific approach discussed earlier in this chapter. The accumulative fragmentalist is one who focuses on defining the personal construct system whereas the constructive alternativist focuses on extension. These are, of course, not mutually exclusive categories. A person may be happier with one approach than the other and may find one more useful in construing certain aspects of life or at certain times in life. What is being described is two different ways of being and relating to the world. One effect of placing choice in the hands of the person is that it makes us in some way responsible for our actions.

Personal Construct Theory Emphasizes the Dialectic

Philosophers have argued long and hard since the days before Aristotle about the advantages and disadvantages of dialectical reasoning and the dialectic process. In its most general sense the dialectic has been defined as:

> any more or less intricate process of conceptual or social conflict, interconnection and change, in which the generation, interpenetration and clash of oppositions, leading to their transcendence in a fuller or more adequate mode of thought or form of life, plays a key role. But the dialectic is itself one of the most complex – and contested – concepts in the story of philosophical and social thought. (Harré and Lamb, 1983: 155)

There are few if any who would argue that personal construct theory is not a dialectical theory. It is so through and through. To start with, it assumes that all constructs are, psychologically speaking, bi-polar. To understand a personal construct one must not only know the basis of *similarity* seen between objects, but must also understand the basis on which they are seen as different. Both similarity and contrast are involved. So we look for the grounds upon which certain matters can be judged as similar to each other and, by the same token, stand in meaningful contrast to certain other objects within the construct's range of convenience. Kelly puts it this way:

> Stated in Hegelian terms this is to say no thesis is complete without its antithesis. Perhaps I should add that I am aware that this dialectical form goes back a good deal further than Hegel, perhaps as far as the pre-Socratic philosopher Anaximander. Be that as it may, I am not so much concerned with the classical logic of the dialectic as I am with its psychological appropriateness in describing how man characteristically functions. (Kelly, 1969b: 169)

Rychlak (1981) suggests it is useful to see the relevance of this by looking at the antithesis of the dialectical reasoning as *demonstrative* reasoning. The demonstrative reasoning of Aristotle says that 'A is not non-A'. A horse is not a non-horse. Kelly points to this being one of the differences between a concept and a construct and why he used the latter. Both involve abstraction. But, in addition, a construct includes a contrast in its abstraction; it contains the notion of a 'percept' in relating to a personal act; and it forms the basis for prediction. In other words, demonstrative reasoning is found in the thinking of the realist – facts are facts. We have to *demonstrate* the basic facts of what we are talking about. Conjecture will not do. The accumulative fragmentalism of Newtonian physics and of science generally was demonstrative well into the early twentieth century.

Kelly gives an example of how he sees use being made of this bi-polarity with a client, and he couples it with the professional construct to do with 'submerged poles' of constructs. The client says 'I believe everything in the world is good. There is nothing bad.'

> The client could have meant several things. She could have meant that everything is now good whereas formerly it was bad. She could have been denying the good–bad dimension as a meaningful dimension and have chosen to do so by asserting the universality of one end of the dimension. She could have meant that everything other than herself was good. Or she could have meant that she was one who saw good in everything whereas others were seers of the bad. As matters turned out, she was expressing her construct in the latter two senses. She meant, 'I suspect that I am bad and I suspect that you see me as bad, even though

> I have the compensating virtue of myself being willing to see everyone as good.' . . .
>
> Perhaps this illustration will suffice, for the time being, to indicate how the Dichotomy Corollary affects the clinician in dealing with his client. Instead of seeing his client as the victim of a submerged conflict between opposing instinctual forces, he sees the dichotomy as an essential feature of thinking itself. As he seeks to understand what his client means, he looks for the elements in the construct context. As long as he approaches man's thinking from the standpoint of formal logic, it is impossible for him to comprehend any thinking which man is unable to verbalize. But as we approach man's thinking psychologically, using both the clinical and the more fragmentary methods of investigation, we can see the operational dichotomization of his constructs into similarities and contrasts. (Kelly, 1991, Vol. 1: 43–4)

In understanding another's construing it is vital to find out what that opposite pole of an important construct is. For only then can there be true understanding. For instance, many clients may have a construct about being *successful.* But those who have its opposite pole as *a failure* or *at peace with the world* or *not yet successful* are living in very different worlds in relation to being *successful.* It equally applies to behaviour. In this case, the question becomes: 'What is my client NOT doing by behaving in this strange way?'

A considerable amount of personal construct theory is based on the Dichotomy Corollary. For example, that central motivational corollary to do with choice says: *We choose for ourselves that alternative in a dichotomized construct through which we anticipate the greater possibility for extension and definition of our system.* 'Here is where inner turmoil so frequently manifests itself. Which shall a man choose, security or adventure? Shall he choose that which leads to immediate certainty or shall he choose that which may eventually give him a wider understanding?' (Kelly, 1991, Vol. 1: 45).

Personal Construct Theory Sees Behaviour as Anticipatory

Kelly makes three mentions in *The Psychology of Personal Constructs* of the influence John Dewey's (1859–1952) thinking had on him. Each one indicates that Kelly saw this influence as being quite profound. On the first occasion he says: 'Dewey emphasised the anticipatory nature of behaviour and the person's use of hypotheses in thinking. The psychology of personal constructs follows Dewey in this respect' (Kelly, 1991, Vol. 1: 90).

Perhaps Kelly's first mention of Dewey is in 'Understandable Psychology', in which he says that Dewey developed William James' functional psychology and that 'Dewey is probably the greatest of living philosophers, at least the greatest of living educational philosophers' (Kelly, 1932: 227).

John Novak (1983) takes an insightful look at the relationship between Kelly and Dewey from the perspective of an educator. Novak quotes Dewey as writing that 'the motive and unspoiled attitude of childhood, marked by ardent curiosity, fertile imagination, and experimental inquiry, is near, very near, to the attitude of the scientific mind' (Dewey, 1933, p. v). Novak points out that the natural tendency to erect, test and reformulate hypotheses is a central theme in Dewey's book *How We Think* (1933) and of his 1938 book *Logic: The Theory of Inquiry*.

Kelly then goes on to explain how he extended Dewey's idea. 'Where Dewey would have said that we understand events through anticipating them, we would add that our lives are wholly oriented towards the anticipation of events. The person moves out towards making more and more of the world predictable and not ordinarily does he withdraw more and more into a predictable world' (1991, Vol. 1: 110).

Novak (1983) sees the main difference here as being Dewey's view that experience is a three-stage affair. The third stage is concerned with linking construing with 'social interactions necessary to maintain and enhance further inquiry'. Novak sees that inquiry 'vitally connected . . . with the social necessity for collective intelligence' (1983: 327): something with which Kelly did not concern himself. The relationship between Kelly's psychology and social construing is discussed in Chapter 4.

Personal Construct Theory Has a Minimum of Explicit or Embedded Values

There is hardly any absolute good and bad behaviour in personal construct theory. That is, there are few good or bad ways of construing, good or bad ways of 'being'. Of course, we as individuals, or we as society, can say quite clearly whether or not a particular way of behaving, construing or experiencing is good or bad. Kelly makes this point when discussing values and knowledge:

> For a long time now, living under the scrutiny of graduate students, I have been kept acutely aware of my limitations in the world of knowledge, but, believe me, I have values. Just what they are has always been somewhat of a secret puzzle to me, but there is no doubt about my having them. In fact, just about every time I start out to do something interesting, there they are! (Kelly, 1959b: 1)

It is the theory itself that is largely value-free. However, to say it 'has no values' is too strong a statement and one that can never be so. The whole of our Western culture is so very value-laden.

Beverly Walker explored Kelly's writings to look for embedded values. She found them linked to the metaphor of 'the scientist'. She says:

> it seems evident that the liberalism inherent in a constructive alternativist stance, although important, is tempered by the emphasis on the importance of making progress. Kelly (1980) articulated his long-term goal of therapy as the rendering 'of aid in this ontological venture.' . . . What Kelly asserted is of significance is that we should continue our search to reach out into what we as yet do not know, sometimes blindly, but at least some of the time with courageous, imaginative daring. This is how we *ought* to be. (Walker, 1992: 268)

Kelly provided psychotherapists with a way of arming themselves against these embedded cultural values. The personal construct psychotherapist is trained to suspend his or her own values and listen only for the client's. It is by no means an easy skill to learn.

For instance, the PCP therapist may hear some puzzling statements when listening to a Hindu client, but these will not pass her by nor be dismissed as irrelevant nor interpreted into Western culture language. Their meaning will lie in the construing of the client.

This will be discussed further later in this chapter when the goals of personal construct therapy and cross-cultural counselling and therapy are studied.

Personal Construct Theory is Reflexive

We know that we think and that we reason. We can turn our mind back on to itself and contemplate our own contemplations. The idea of reflexivity is central to the whole of Kelly's thinking.

Surprising as it may seem, many psychologists have found this difficult to encompass within their theories and research. The most powerful influence on the rejection of our powers for reflection have been the behaviourists, especially J. B. Watson and more recently B. F. Skinner. These theorists and experimentalists found human consciousness, thinking and feeling incompatible with their notions of science. The extreme form of this was expressed by Watson in 1913:

> Psychology as the behaviorist views it is a purely objective experimental branch of natural science. Its theoretical goal is the prediction and control of behavior. Introspection forms no essential part of its methods, nor is the scientific value of its data dependent upon the readiness with

> which they lend themselves to interpretation in terms of consciousness. The behaviorist, in his efforts to get a unitary scheme of animal response, recognizes no dividing line between man and brute. (Watson, 1913: 158)

It is worth bearing in mind that it was in a climate such as this that Kelly started learning his psychology.

The issue was still around in psychology in 1962, when Oliver and Landfield published their paper 'Reflexivity: an unfaced issue of psychology'. And in 1966 Bannister addressed a group of American psychologists and pointed out that the ability to be reflexive prevents psychologists from diminishing our personal concepts of ourselves. He said:

> At a joke level psychologists may argue that a particular psychoanalyst is writing a particular paper in order to sublimate his sex instinct, or we may toy with the notion that a book by some learning theorist is evidence that the said learning theorist was suffering from a build-up of reactive inhibition. But in our more solemn moments we seem to prefer the paradoxical view that psychologists are explainers, predictors, and experimenters, whereas the organism, God bless him, is a very different kettle of fish. . . . The delight and instruction which many of us find in George Kelly's Personal Construct Theory derives in no small measure from the fact that it is an explicitly reflexive theory. There may be no onus on the chemist when he writes his papers on the nature of acids and alkalis to account in terms of his acid–alkali distinction for his behaviour in writing a journal paper. But psychologists are in no such fortunate position.
>
> Turning this issue of reflexivity the other way around, I am reminded of a recurrent theme in certain types of science fiction story. The master-chemist has finally produced a bubbling green slime in his test tubes, the potential of which is great but the properties of which are mysterious. He sits alone in his laboratory, test tube in hand, brooding about what to do with the bubbling green slime. Then it slowly dawns on him that the bubbling green slime is sitting alone in the test tube brooding about what to do with him. This special nightmare of the chemist is the permanent work-a-day world of the psychologist – the bubbling green slime is always wondering what to do with you. (Bannister, 1966: 21–2)

Reflexivity, of course, has implications of profound importance for the practice and teaching of psychotherapy. Personal construct psychotherapy is a learning experience for the client. He or she will be learning how to become a more competent personal scientist. The psychotherapist will be assisting this process by showing the client some of the ways in which they can go about the task.

Personal construct psychotherapy takes place in the context of the interaction between client and therapist. That interaction is one in which the therapist both interacts with the client on the basis of a provisional *knowing* (by subsuming) the client's personal construing of the world, and later makes observations about the client, *knowing* that his or her own constructions are involved in these observations. The psychotherapeutic relationship is discussed in more detail later in this chapter.

The student of personal construct psychotherapy has to learn about the theory and practice both in academic and experiential terms. In gaining this personal experiential knowing, the student and the client come to understand the truly reflexive nature of Kelly's theory.

Summary

Kelly's contributions to the theory of psychotherapy are the same as his contributions to psychology generally. He put forward ideas that profoundly altered our views of the person and, hence, the client.

The client is a self-created form of motion who comes to accept some responsibility for who they are and who seeks to change that being. The client is a whole person whose passions and thoughts are not kept in separate compartments. The client's behaviours are personal experiments that are designed to test out the current 'best guesses' of his or her current understanding of the world. They also give some indication of what the client is NOT doing by behaving as they are now doing. The client is not trapped by these current understandings because there are always alternatives available – however difficult they may be to grasp.

THEORETICAL CONTRIBUTIONS TO PRACTICE

Having looked at the theory of psychotherapy from a personal construct perspective, this section deals with George Kelly's contribution to the more specific context within which psychotherapy takes place. Chapter 3 deals with contributions made by Kelly to the way in which psychotherapists actually go about the practice of psychotherapy.

The Medical Model and Kelly's Alternative

Historically, the 'medical model' of psychological problems came into being in the early nineteenth century when the medical profession took over the the 'treatment' of those thought to be 'mad'.

Kelly developed most of his ideas in the 1930s and 1940s when the medical model was almost universally accepted as the only way to view those with psychological problems. As Brendan Maher has pointed out in Chapter 1, clinical psychologists were working very definitely within the medical context. The power-base was medical. Doctors insisted they were responsible for the 'treatment' of 'patients'. Someone 'diagnosed' as being 'mentally ill' was therefore a 'patient' and, consequently, a doctor's responsibility. But Kelly's early work with his children's travelling clinic gave him a freedom of action unknown to most psychologists. Kelly's active participation in the development of clinical psychology as an independent profession has been detailed in Chapter 1.

In *The Psychology of Personal Constructs* Kelly was arguing against the idea that the medical term 'therapy' should be applied to the 'treatment' of the 'patient'. His central point was that it is not usually fruitful to transfer ideas from one area of application – that is, medicine – to another – that is, psychology. There are exceptions such as the inter-change of ideas between physicists and psychologists resulting in work on cybernetics and servo-mechanisms. He goes on to say:

> It is only in certain cases, such as professional medicine's attempt to preempt the field of psychiatry, that the invasion has introduced misanthropic elements of intellectual dictatorship and the suppression of free research. (Kelly 1991, Vol. 1: 129)

But language changes slowly and medical words survive. Kelly said that he had thought of substituting the word *reconstruction* for the word *therapy* since the ultimate objective of the enterprise is *the psychological reconstruction of life*. 'If it had not been such a mouth-filling word we might have gone ahead with the idea. Perhaps later we may!' (Kelly, 1991, Vol. 1: 130). But he stresses that one sometimes has to use familiar words for communication purposes, and 'therapy' is one such word. He also tried to replace the word 'patient' with the Rogerian alternative 'client' – but not always successfully.

This battle against the involvement of medicine with psychological problems was popularized by the psychiatrist Thomas Szasz in the 1960s. There was first his paper 'The myth of mental illness' published in the journal *American Psychologist* in 1960 and then his book *The Myth of Mental Illness: foundations of a theory of personal conduct* in 1961. He was followed a little later by such people as the sociologist Goffman with his book *Asylums* (1968) and the psychiatrist R. D. Laing (1967).

Szasz's argument went deeply into the issue, pointing out the fundamental problems involved in the use of the medical model. One of the clearest underlying assumptions of the concept of mental illness is that the person is not responsible for his or her deviant behaviour. Szasz argued that the concept of mental illness is a myth.

Historically, many ideas to explain the inexplicable have been seen, not as theories, but as self-evident causes of the events; for example, concepts of witches, instincts and gods. Szasz said that mental illness is a myth in that sense and has outlived its usefulness. To him, those deemed to be mentally ill are better seen as deviating from some social norm. At present, these deviant behaviours are first described in psychosocial, ethical or legal terms and then 'corrected' by medical practitioners using medical concepts and methods.

Szasz's model is that people have *problems with living* rather than being *mentally ill.* For finding the problems of living more overwhelming than most, the person should not be taken out of society and put into a mental hospital. The social reality of such action is still today what it was centuries ago – 'punishment without trial, imprisonment without time limit, and stigmatisation without hope of redress' (Szasz, 1969: 57).

Kelly was not greatly impressed by *The Myth of Mental Illness.* His review of the Szasz book was entitled 'Muddles, myths and medicine'. In that review Kelly says:

> Hereabouts lies the reason for this reviewer's faint feelings of disappointment. He would like to go all-out in support of a treatise that debunks mental illness – both 'mental' and 'illness'. But the author accepts both constructs. His thesis is merely that they do not go together, that what is mental cannot be illness, and what is illness cannot be mental. (Kelly, 1962: 264)

Jonathan Raskin and Franz Epting (1993) point to one problem with the Szasz model. To emphasize seeing people as having *problems of living* instead of a *mental illness* is not compatible with the biological model associated with *Diagnostic and Statistical Manual of Mental Disorders* (DSM) categories. This details the agreed groupings into which psychiatrists insert people and their problems. It is the psychiatrist's blueprint of psychological disorder.

Kelly made clear his dislike of the DSM categorical system. He says that to start out calling a client 'schizoid' is fair enough. But it is *unprofessional* for a therapist to continue thinking of the client primarily as a schizophrenic.

> No client should continue looking like a stereotype to an alert therapist who works with him day after day.
>
> For the most part it is misleading to think of a disorder solely in terms of a disease entity. That makes one dependent upon a published catalogue of 'disorders'. If a client's construction does not fit one of the official categories, his actual difficulties are likely to be ignored. (Kelly, 1991, Vol. 2: 195)

One of the essential features of the arguments of both Kelly and Szasz is that all people are, in some sense, responsible for their actions; they have freedom of choice. The mental illness label both denies them responsibility for their actions and denies them choice. Kelly and Szasz think that we may trap ourselves by our own ways of construing events, but that it is always possible to find alternative ways of looking at things. No one says this is necessarily easy, but both feel that we have no mandate to deny other human beings the right to choice and the right to take responsibility for their actions. 'Man can enslave himself with his own ideas and then win his freedom again by reconstruing life' (Kelly, 1991, Vol. 1: 15).

There are other aspects of the medical model that people have found problematic. For instance, Watzlawick says:

> As is known, the traditional psychiatric criterion for a person's sanity or insanity is the degree of his 'reality adaptation'. This criterion tacitly assumes that there is such a thing as a real, objective reality and that it is open to our scrutiny and understanding. It goes without saying that the irruption of constructivist thinking into the orthodoxy of this view of reality is producing severe repercussions in that discipline and its institutions that are considered competent for the diagnosis and treatment of madness. (Watzlawick, 1984: 66–7)

He sees one of the great problems as being the fact that we have very sketchy definitions of mental health, yet we are prepared to have categories of abnormal behaviour that are 'perfected to the last detail' (p. 105). He sees this as making it extremely easy to have self-fulfilling prophecies. 'The essential part of the self-fulfilling effect of psychiatric diagnoses is based on our unshakable conviction that everything that has a name must *therefore* actually exist' (p. 106). David Rosenhan (1984) describes an experiment in which people with no obvious psychological problem got themselves admitted to psychiatric hospitals. They were generally accepted as patients. For instance, they all took extensive notes of what was happening and did this quite publicly. Hardly any were questioned. None of the staff paid any attention to all this writing, and all the elaborate precautions the pseudo-patients were prepared to take to prevent any being read were unnecessary. Three of the pseudo-patients saw nurses' records and one had written 'patient engages in writing behaviour'. The whole account, however 'unscientific', makes disturbing reading. This is also in line with Szasz's later thinking (1970).

That brief discussion of the medical model leads directly into the nature of Kelly's views of diagnosis. It is in dealing with 'diagnosis' that Kelly spells out his alternative to the medical model.

The Nature of 'Diagnosis'

As with the term 'therapy' so Kelly kept the term 'diagnosis' for communication purposes. Kelly's theory leads therapist and counsellor to strive to understand the client's understanding of the world, whereas the medical practitioner strives to categorize the client's behaviour and language.

Kelly uses the concept of 'transitive diagnosis'.

> The term suggests we are concerned with transitions in the client's life, that we are looking for bridges between the client's present and his future. Moreover, we expect to take an active part in helping the client select or build the bridges to be used and in helping him cross them safely. The client does not ordinarily sit cooped up in a nosological pigeonhole; he proceeds along his way. If the psychologist expects to help him he must get up off his chair and start moving along with him. (Kelly, 1991, Vol. 2: 153)

Diagnosis becomes the planning stage of therapy. And, because the person is constantly changing, transitive diagnoses are constantly being revised. The aim is to up-date constantly the understanding of how the client construes the world and his or her problem. Methods that may be used to assist in the process of arriving at transitive diagnoses are given in the next chapter.

The obvious important difference between Kelly's approach and that of psychiatry is that the problem is formulated in terms of the client's construing of the world and not in terms of the world of medicine's construing. Personal construct psychotherapy is totally idiographic in the sense that it deals with the unique perspective on the world of one individual. It is the opposite of the nomothetic view of medicine which says that all psychological disturbances can be grouped in such a way that all individuals displaying those disturbances can be put into the same specific category.

Only by coming to an understanding of the client's construing system can a tentative plan of therapy be worked out. It is tentative because it has to be put to the test. The reflexive nature of personal construct theory says that the clinician is as much a scientist as is the client. The clinician has to test out his or her own hypotheses based on the transitive diagnosis. They may be supported, in which case the client and therapist can move forward. If not, then it is back to the drawing-board.

Kelly thus gave the psychotherapy process an evolutionary quality. The issues that form its focus, and the methods used, change as the process evolves.

A Subsystem of Professional Constructs

To carry out the work leading to a transitive diagnosis, Kelly provides the psychotherapist with a complex subsystem of *professional* constructs:

> These professional constructs do not refer to disease entities, or to types of people or to traits. They are proposed as universal axes with respect to which it is possible to plot any person's behavior, at any time or at any place. They are also axes with respect to which it is possible to plot the changes that occur in a person's psychological processes. In themselves, they are neither good nor bad, healthy nor unhealthy, adaptive nor maladaptive. They are like the points of the compass; they are simply assumed in order to enable one to plot relative positions and chart courses of movement. (Kelly, 1991, Vol. 1: 335)

As you might expect, he was at pains to point out that these professional constructs are propositional as opposed to 'nothing but' categories.

> They are designed to subsume at a comparatively high level of abstraction, and with great permeability, the complex shadings of meaning that one encounters in his clients' personal construct systems. (Kelly, 1991, Vol. 1: 134)

It is not necessary to detail all the professional constructs here, since this is not a personal construct psychotherapy cookbook. Those chosen are commonly used in the practice of personal construct psychotherapy.

Levels of Cognitive Awareness – An Alternative to 'the Unconscious'

Kelly was not happy with the psychodynamic notion of psychic energy and unconscious processes. However, he was only too well aware that much goes on in ourselves which we cannot get a hook into so as to help us describe what it is. As discussed earlier in this chapter, personal construct theory sees the person as being alive and kicking, so no explanation based on energy systems or dynamics is necessary to propel us into action.

Kelly preferred to talk about *construing at differing levels of cognitive awareness*, ranging from high to low, rather than an entity of 'the unconscious'. A high level of awareness is what is going on as you try to understand what I am trying to say. A less high level of awareness occurs if you read something that disturbs you or makes you angry or otherwise makes your autonomic nervous system come into play. That could happen if what I am saying has some deeper meaning for you. For instance, if you are a counsellor or psychotherapist, what you read might seem to question your current ways of understanding your clients. You might feel Kellyian threat if you were to accept what I am saying. Such a conclusion might imply that you had to change much of your psychotherapeutic practice – a somewhat daunting task.

At the lowest level of cognitive awareness there is the *preverbal construct*. That is, a construct which continues to be used, even though it has no consistent word symbols. It may or may not have been devised before the person had command of speech. This concept plays a very important part in personal construct psychotherapy. As with other theoretical systems of psychotherapy, one task is to help the client attach some verbal labels to these preverbal constructs so that they can be looked at, mulled over and generally made sense of.

It is important to note that the preverbal construct has no 'psychic energy' trying to force it into consciousness. It is a discrimination to be 'taken out' of the person's repertoire of constructs when it appears useful for ordering events in the present.

For example, a child has a preverbal personal construct that all 'mothers' are *soft and cuddly* whereas 'non-mothers' are not. This non-verbal way of discriminating between the women with whom he comes into contact is related to how he behaves. He runs up to and cuddles 'mothers' and holds back from the others. In the years to come, he never finds it necessary to elaborate and verbalize that construct. It remains with him in its original form. In adult life he uses it whenever *cuddly* women cross his path. Some people might attribute to him the motive of seeking a 'mother figure'. But in his terms he is seeking all the childhood security, feelings of warmth and satiation that accompanied the original discrimination. It might only become a problem for him if he were to marry a *cuddly* woman who changed into a *non-cuddly* one.

The preverbal construct of a precocious child, perhaps one whose speech has been delayed, may pose special problems for the therapist. Such a client may make statements such as: 'You couldn't understand. Nobody can understand. It's no use my trying to explain.' As an intelligent child such a client may have understood a considerable amount that was going on around him but, with delayed language, had no words with which to tie those experiences down.

Preverbal constructs are sometimes 'acted out'. That is, the constructs are brought into play by behaving. This type of behaving is decried in some therapies, but little is good or bad in an absolute sense for the personal construct therapist. 'Acting out' is certainly not seen as undesirable. How can we apply a personal construct with no words to tie it down, except by behaving it? The difficult task for the therapist is to understand what constructions that behaviour is testing out and who the other characters involved are.

These preverbal personal constructs are often to do with dependency. As infants we depend on others for our survival and any construing at that time may well have a sense of urgency about it. Dependency constructs are not only preverbal, they are also 'core'. They are to do with the infant's maintenance processes, its survival. Because of this, we should not expect a client who is using preverbal constructs to deal with the adult world to behave at all times like an adult. 'The therapist has before him an infant who is speaking with the voice of an adult. The infant's thinking may be overlaid with the sophistication of adulthood; but as the overlay is thrown back, the wide-eyed, vaguely comprehending child is revealed' (Kelly, 1991, Vol. 1: 341).

Kelly argues that everyone is dependent on others throughout their lives. What happens is that these dependency constructs become more open to new people. There was once only one mother on whom everything depended. But as the child grows, they discover that other people can supply their needs. The dependencies thus become dispersed.

Kelly relates preverbal construing to psychosomatic complaints. The client has typically responded with this physical behaviour over the years, perhaps as far back as the early years when dependent on others for satisfaction of all needs. When similar events are construed as occurring in adult life, this behaviour is again brought into play. A situation has aroused dependency core construing that requires urgent attention. The person responds as he or she did as an infant. In such cases, it is often necessary for the therapist to encourage some dependency in the relationship so that this construing has a hope of being given verbal anchors.

Another form of construing at a low level of cognitive awareness is *submergence* of a construct pole. The importance of the bi-polarity of constructs in Kelly's system has been discussed earlier in this chapter together with an example of submergence. Submerged poles can cause problems in therapy because of the difficulty of elaborating them. If the therapist finds she is going round and round in circles with the client, she might check to be sure she has that elusive opposite pole identified.

Ways of Construing Feelings

Kelly relates feelings to awareness that one's construing system is in transition. The ones he specified as being vital for the process of psychotherapy are *anxiety, threat and guilt.* In addition there is *hostility*, which is shown behaviourally, and can be a response to threat and may be connected with guilt. In fact, it is probable that they never occur in pure culture. Here is an example of where Kelly did not create new words for his new definitions, but redefined existing words. He points out that you have these two courses of action when you want to put forward a new idea – redefine or create new words – and neither is ideal.

Anxiety is defined by Kelly as an awareness that the spectacles we have created over the years to make sense of all that confronts us are in need of extension to help us interpret what is happening. In simple terms, a sound in the dark causes anxiety because we cannot be sure whether it is a burglar, a cat knocking off the dustbin lid, or a fire. Once we have construed it one way or the other we can act. Before then we are impotent.

Within the system Kelly created, we are anxious most of the time. As he puts it:

> from the standpoint of the psychology of personal constructs, anxiety, *per se*, is not to be classified as either good or bad. It represents the awareness that one's construction system does not apply to the events at hand. It is, therefore, a precondition for making revisions. (Kelly, 1991, Vol. 1: 367)

Anxiety plays a major role in the transitive diagnoses and in the psychotherapy process itself. In his paper 'The psychology of the unknown' (1977) Kelly points out that we are always striving to grasp a reality but 'What we think we know is anchored only in our own assumptions, not in the bed rock of truth itself, and that world we seek to understand remains always on the horizons of our thoughts' (1977: 6) – an example of Kelly's fascination with what lies beyond the horizon? He is saying that there is everyday anxiety. But this is at the opposite extreme to that of the client who cannot make sense of who she is or what is happening to her. That client may well experience intense anxiety nearly all the time. Identifying areas of anxiety in the client's construing system gives important pointers to where elaboration or reconstruction are required.

Threat is defined as the awareness that we are facing imminent, comprehensive change in our core structures. The perceived potential change is vast. Threat is an ever-present possibility in successful psychotherapy. The client sees at some level of awareness that, if she continues this movement, she will soon have changed radically in ways that do not yet make personal sense – she could not live that person – and there might be no return. So she 'relapses' or resists further change. This is dealt with more fully later in this chapter.

Threat can usefully be understood in relation to one of the ways in which we and our clients deal with threatening circumstances – we can become hostile. *Hostility* is a very useful concept in therapy and is defined as 'the continued effort to extort validational evidence in favour of a type of social prediction which has already been recognised as a failure' at some level of awareness. We try to force our experiences to fit how we construe things. It is said to occur when we 'make' an event happen to support our prediction even though, at some level of awareness, we know we are on to a loser. For instance, the person in successful therapy gets threatened by the speed of change and calls a halt by becoming hostile. 'You know how much better I have been over these past few weeks. Well, I realise now that it is because my manager has been away on maternity leave. She is back now. So, you see, everything is as it was. I have not really changed at all.'

Such *hostility* is used by all of us, just as we all experience anxiety. But the identification of areas of hostility in psychotherapy is vital. For one thing, it shows where change is likely to be resisted. Being reflexive, it is also necessary to say that psychotherapists need to be on the lookout for hostility in themselves in their behaviour towards their client. For example, 'I said this client will improve and I will continue therapy until she does!'

When you see a theme in a client's life constantly repeating itself, look for the hostility. There is then an adage that says: 'Where there is hostility, look for the *guilt*.' For instance, consider someone who says they are unable to sustain a lasting relationship with anyone. The question becomes 'How would this client construe herself if she were to be someone who *could* sustain a lasting relationship?' Over the years, all her attempts have failed. Her core role may be of someone who *cannot* have a lasting relationship and she has to make sure that the evidence keeps coming in to validate that notion. Until she is able to construe herself differently, she must maintain the *status quo*.

We experience *guilt* when we become aware of doing something that violates some core way in which we see ourselves. Guilt is a good example of the way in which personal construct theory is free of obvious values. The psychopath can be said to experience guilt when he lets a person off the hook at the end of his confidence trick. As an example of guilt in practice, take the wife who has fallen out of love with her husband. But she sees herself as a good wife and good wives love their husbands. The idea of not loving him is unacceptable to her – she would experience considerable *guilt*. So she becomes *hostile*. Unfortunately, her husband *will* persist in behaving like a good husband, but she is in the business of showing to herself that he is the one who is bad – he is a bad husband. He brings her flowers, she says he must have a guilty conscience. She goes on about his unfaithfulness (of which she has no objective evidence) until he shouts back. She uses this shouting as evidence that he is a bad husband. She has extorted evidence to show that her construing of him is correct. She is preserving her core role of herself as a good (but wronged) wife by behaving in a hostile manner. Guilt is powerful because of its relationship with core role construing and one's 'maintenance processes'. Kelly changed the saying about sin to read that sometimes 'the wages of guilt is death'.

Loose and Tight Construing

The professional constructs of *tight* and *loose* construing are to do with process rather than content. A tight construct is one which leads to unvarying predictions and a loose construct is one which leads to varying predictions but which retains its identity.

Extreme examples of loose construing can be seen in dreaming and poetry. In the world of psychological disturbance it describes the type of thought process found in some people diagnosed as schizophrenic where the whole thread of thought is like shifting sand. This type of thought process disorder was, at one time, likened to surrealist painting. But the difference is that the painter can put down his or her brush and go and give a lucid talk on his art whereas the schizophrenic person has lost the ability to tighten their construing and so deal predictably with their world.

I want to stress that Kelly is not talking here about a trait. We are not classified for all time as either tight or loose construers. At one time we may find it useful to construe in a relatively tight way and at another time in a loose way. We will probably find it useful to use some parts of our system for making sense of the world in a loose way – perhaps when listening to music – and some in a tight way. When we have consumed enough alcohol to be placed in the category of 'tight', we will probably be construing in a fairly loose way. When being interviewed for a job we will probably be doing our best to construe things tightly so as to ensure maximum control over what we are about.

This dimension is important as an interim goal of psychotherapy. The client needs to be able to use the shifting from loose to tight construing and back again because this is the creativity cycle, discussed in the following section.

Although there are more professional constructs, we have moved irrevocably into theoretical aspects of the psychotherapeutic process.

The Psychotherapy Process and the Nature of Change

Essential theoretical underpinnings of the psychotherapy process are the 'cycles'. These are to do with creativity, experience and decision-making.

The Experience Cycle

As has been said, but can perhaps never be repeated too often, construing is about experiencing. We are seen as a totality and a process, proceeding through life trying to make sense of the events that impinge upon us. The experience cycle starts with anticipation and ends with reconstruction and has three stages in between. Kelly's description of the experience cycle was elaborated several years after the publication of his two volumes in 1955.

Kelly binds the whole venture of psychotherapy to the experience cycle. We *anticipate* what may happen if we explore ourselves as being, for example, *friendly* rather than *frightened of people*. We then *commit* ourselves to the experiments likely to be involved; there is then the *encounter* between oneself and the experience. We have committed ourselves to being open to what may happen in this encounter; now we are able to see whether the events we have encountered *confirm or disconfirm* our anticipations. It is not just that we are looking to see whether we are right or wrong in our expectations. It is the process that matters. The cycle of experience involves the experiment itself.

In that experience cycle, the philosophy of constructive alternativism and much else besides is bound in three crucial notions. One is that each one of us has created ourselves and can therefore re-create if we do not like the current model. A second is that we have choice. The third is the notion of taking responsibility for what we do.

The Creativity Cycle

A working, experiential knowledge of the creativity cycle of construing is essential for a personal construct psychotherapist. As mentioned in relation to the thought process disorder found in some of those diagnosed as schizophrenic, the cycle is between tight and loose construing.

> A person who always uses tight constructions may be productive – that is, he may turn out a lot of things – but he cannot be creative; he cannot produce anything which has not already been blue-printed. Creativity always arises out of preposterous thinking. If the creative person mumbles the first part of his Creativity Cycle out loud, he is likely to get sharp criticism from everyone who is within earshot. For this reason

> most creative persons keep their loose constructions in the earlier part of their Creativity Cycle to themselves. This is not hard to do, since these loose constructions are often preverbal in nature anyway. (Kelly, 1991, Vol. 1: 388)

The whole of the psychotherapy encounter is seen as a creative process which involves a series of creativity cycles. But as we have seen, tight and loose construing can be issues in themselves for the client and form part of the subsystem of professional constructs.

Only by maintaining a cycle between tight construing and loose construing can creativity flourish. If a person has lost the ability to tighten their construing they are left in a world in which they cannot make workable predictions about their fellows. If a person is unable to loosen their ways of construing they are fixed in an unchanging and relatively unchangeable world; all change is fraught with danger. To deal with life's uncertainties, we need to be able to move from one way of construing to another.

The CPC Decision-making Cycle

This is to do with choice linked to decision-making. First there is the stage of *circumspection* (C). We consider the various options open to us. An important aspect of this stage is that if it is foreshortened, the person will behave *impulsively*. After circumspecting, we *pre-empt* (P) or decide how we are going to construe the issue. Having decided that the options are either *to knock this man down for his insulting behaviour* or *to walk away*, we choose (C) which pole of the construct we are going to commit ourselves to.

The person who acts impulsively is not showing lack of control. They are using control in the sense that they have made a choice in the CPC cycle, but they have done it very quickly. Clients will often show impulsivity during a period of reconstruing. Alternative courses of action are not considered before the choice is made to experiment with some new behaviour. While it may be of value if it takes place in the therapy session, it can cause problems outside the confines of the therapy room. But it is a risk the therapist must take if the client is to collect evidence of the new constructions. The therapist therefore must guide the experimentations carefully and not show impulsivity himself.

There are other ways in which we may not complete the cycle satisfactorily. We can have trouble making the final choice and so delay completing the cycle at all. The extreme example of this would be the obsessional client who finds it impossible to decide whether to turn the door-handle or not. He has pre-empted the construct *to turn the handle versus not turn the handle* but cannot choose to which pole of the construct he should commit himself. Such clients suffer great anguish and psychotherapists who feel they have the skills to help such a person are rare.

Some of the Skills Required of the Therapist

Several of the skills a personal construct psychotherapist requires are the same as those for many other therapies. But there are a few that may be somewhat different and all stem directly from personal construct theory and its philosophy.

Suspending and Subsuming

It is under the system of professional constructs that the psychotherapist must *subsume* the client's construing system; that is, look at the client's world through the professional constructs and not through personal constructs. In order to do this, the psychotherapist must have learned the skill of *suspending* their own construing system.

Suspension is putting into practice the art of subsuming the client's construing system within the system of 'professional constructs'. To do this, the therapist has to be able to suspend his or her own personal, value-laden construing system.

That may sound easy. But it is a skill many find hard to achieve. It basically means that if you are a strong believer in socialism you have no problem with listening to the personal values of a staunch conservative – you have suspended your socialist values. Or, if you are a woman and a strong believer in the equality of men and women, you will have no problem with helping someone reconstrue life who is a 'male chauvinist pig' and lets you know he thinks women are inferior beings. That may be asking a little too much. But it is an ideal. In practice, personal construct practitioners are required to develop the skill to such an extent that, on the rare occasion when they are caught unawares, they know what is happening and quickly and consciously suspend those values. *The client's values are all that matter.*

Credulous Listening

Most important of all, the therapist takes care not to 'interpret' anything the client says in the initial stages of therapy. *The therapist could well be wrong.* The therapist may have some knowledge that tells her that the client is lying. But that is of no consequence if the therapist is listening credulously.

This credulous approach means the therapist simply makes a mental note of the context in which the lie occurred and accepts it.

The point of interest for the therapist is why the client wishes to tell an untruth. The credulous approach helps establish an early relationship of trust and, it is hoped, conveys respect for the client and acceptance by, and involvement of, the therapist.

It should be noted that the personal construct psychotherapist will not be credulous throughout the therapy. Far from it. There will be times when it is important to challenge the client, for instance. But Kelly suggests the therapist should adopt the credulous approach during the early stages of therapy.

Being credulous does not simply mean being empathic. The therapist will be of no use to the client if he or she simply gets immersed in the client's construing of the world and the problem. That would seriously interfere with the use the therapist might be to the client. In being credulous, the psychotherapist is being empathic while *at the same time* subsuming (understanding) the client's world within the system of professional constructs.

Creativity

Kelly points out that a personal construct psychotherapist needs to be able to create methods, approaches and activities with the client that may not have been used before. In other words, the therapist should not feel they are restricted by a tool-bag of methods and ready-made formulas to help the client change. He explains therapeutic creativity thus:

> Creativity implies that one can construe elements as being alike and different in ways which are not logically deduced or, as yet, literally defined. Creation is therefore an act of daring, an act of daring through which the creator abandons those literal defenses behind which he might hide if his act is questioned or its results proven invalid. The psychotherapist who dares not try anything he cannot verbally defend is likely to be sterile in a psychotherapeutic relationship. (Kelly, 1991, Vol. 2: 32)

The Relationship With the Client

The relationship is spelled out by Kelly as one between supervisor and research student. The client (research student) comes with the subject to be studied and they are the expert on the topic chosen. The therapist (research supervisor) is the expert on the methods that might be used, the process of change, and on the design of experiments that might be helpful to the client.

The important feature here is that the client is considered to be the expert. The client has the ultimate solution to the problem. The therapist claims no special knowledge or expertise that will be a short-cut to 'freedom' for the client. However, there are, of course, some generalizations that can be made from experience with several people who have the same problem: for example, those who have experienced sex abuse as children (Cummins, 1992; Harter and Neimeyer, 1995); those who stutter (Fransella, 1972); those who are depressed (for example, Rowe, 1983) and so on. Ultimately, though, the client has a problem that has unique qualities and is approached as such.

Kelly's redefinition of the notion of 'role' is central here. As was mentioned in Chapter 1, it is to do with stepping inside another's shoes and looking at the world through that other's eyes. Kelly spells out how his definition of role differs from others in the following excerpt from an interview:

> there are three notions of role here. The oldest notion being of a course of activity articulated with the activity of others; that notion could be tied up with the notion of man as an economic entity or 'economic man'. The more recent notion of man as surrounded by a set of expectations, a notion that would undergird a society which saw itself composed of ideologies; this would relate to a notion of 'ideological man' or man who conformed to ideas or ideologies. Then, with all the emphasis on psychotherapy that is going on saying that if you have a problem it is not so much something you should try to solve but is something you should go and lie down to be treated for. This could be, if it catches on in all the strata of our society, then I suppose you could say that it would bring on a society of self-conscious man. But if we follow the notion of role from construct theory we might develop the notion of man or a society composed of empathic man or *inquiring man*. Understanding coming from active inquiry using their own behaviour not as something to act out but as a means of understanding their world. Understanding by adventure as was characteristic of the humanistic century 1450 to 1550. It strikes me as a century that has some of the characteristics which we might hope to recover. (Kelly, 1966)

Kelly's definition of role does not involve necessary acceptance of what the client says or does; it does not involve any value judgements; it means solely that when we attempt to look at the world through the client's goggles, we are playing a role in relation to that client. But this is a two-way process – the client has to try to understand what the therapist is about. There is an expectation that the therapist as well as the client will change during the therapy process.

Transference

As with the concept of 'the unconscious', Kelly acknowledges that something that can usefully be called transference may well take place between client and therapist, but he disagreed with the psychoanalytic interpretation of it. He does not see it as something that necessarily has to be 'worked through'.

What Kelly does agree with is the idea that the client has to construe the therapist in some way or other. The client has to try to understand how the therapist is seeing the world – including the client herself. After all, the only way we can hope to understand anyone else is by developing a role relationship with them – by construing their construction processes. In therapy, the client uses her existing role constructs and peers at the therapist through them. She may try several on for size. What she sees is the answer to the question 'What is transference?'

Part of the psychotherapist's job is to find out how they are construed by the client. These constructions will change from time to time. They can become negative. Perhaps the therapist has threatened the client. Perhaps the client is using the therapist in order to work out some preverbal hatred. Kelly says:

> the behaviour of the client may indicate that he now sees the therapeutic situation as one in which the 'negative' construct can safely be brought to light. The therapist has been successful in producing a laboratory situation which enables the client to invoke such a construct. At last the client brings his delinquent construct into the laboratory, alive and kicking, for a preliminary test. Here is what the therapist may have been looking for. (Kelly, 1991, Vol. 2: 76)

The very nature of the therapeutic setting, with the acceptance of confidences by one person from another, invites being construed in a stereotyped way. For instance, being construed in the 'father figure' role means the therapist may also be construed in a fixed way along other constructs – perhaps as *domineering*, *stern* and so forth. It is difficult for the therapist to move the client on from these stereotypes.

Another aspect of the transferring of these stereotypical constructs on to the therapist is that they are often preverbal dependency constructs. The types of dependency constructs clients place on their therapists vary in the needs requiring to be satisfied. Some therapies and some therapists encourage dependency transference. But the personal construct therapist does not. Because the relationship is a partnership, dependency is minimized. However, if the client is unable to start the reconstruction process because there is such a wealth of preverbal construing, the therapist may decide that to allow dependency to develop is the only way in which to start.

Kelly describes two types of transference *secondary* and *primary*. Secondary transference is one in which the client uses a variety of constructs in the attempt to understand the therapist. He is *tall* like father, *kindly* like mother and *wise* like Uncle John. No real problems here.

In primary transference, the client construes the therapist pre-emptively. The therapist is seen as *nothing but* the wisest man in the world. The therapist has been typecast and is in a conceptual strait-jacket. The client becomes attached to the therapist in a primary and dependent way.

Thus, for Kelly, transference is a form of construing on the part of the client which the therapist has to try to understand, along with the client's construing in other areas. It holds no special place. It requires no special rules. One result of this is the fact that personal construct psychotherapy need not, and seldom does, last for years.

Interpretation

Interpretations made by the therapist of the client's behaviour play such a major role in some psychotherapies that it may seem remarkable to know that Kelly would have none of them. However, when it is stated that 'All interpretations understood by the client are perceived in terms of his own system' it becomes clearer. It is always the client who does the interpreting and not the therapist.

This does not mean that the therapist never gives his or her own views. But they only do so if they think it will help the client reconstrue. The most usual way of expressing an opinion is to put it in the form of a question such as 'It seems to me that you are saying . . . Am I right in that?' It will be no surprise to know that Kelly had a good deal to say on how to facilitate interpretation in the client, and he gave three lectures on the subject (Kelly, 1959b).

The Goals of Psychotherapy

Kelly spells out his view of the goals for the client in his paper 'The psychology of optimal man'.

> In presenting the goals of psychotherapy as we see them we have laid initial stress on man as a creature who forges his own destiny rather than allows himself to drift with the tide of human affairs. The term 'personal constructs' refers to the guidelines by which he pinpoints anticipated events and along which he establishes the dimensions of the freedom he hopes to exercise and the pathways of movement he seeks to follow. There are many interesting processes man uses in reaching his ends, some of which we have attempted to describe. All of them fall within the purview of the technically versatile psychotherapist.
>
> Man uses many kinds of resources too. One of the resources men occasionally find useful is a psychotherapist. And – speaking of therapists – in addition to the goals his client ought to seek, the therapist

needs to have a goal of his own; he ought to try to be made good use of. (Kelly, 1980: 35)

Kelly looks at goals, as one might expect, in terms of process rather than ultimate achievements. There are no 'self-actualizations' or, for example, 'where id once was now ego shall be' or 'becoming oneself'. He argues that to try to 'become oneself' assumes there is a 'true' self hidden among the present mess. Gaining insight is a concept that implies coming face to face with something that has been hiding there all the time – some 'truth'. It is not. We are that person we have created and we are a person that currently makes the most sense. What we do all have is amazing potential. But only we can find it by stretching and extending ourselves out into the unknown. Our potential can only be discovered by questioning ourselves and challenging our previous notions of what our limitations are. We 'set out to be what we are not . . . to render and utilize technical aid in this ontological venture is the special transaction we call *psychotherapy*' (Kelly, 1980: 20). The optimally functioning person is open to the evidence with which his experience confronts him.

One of the goals of personal construct psychotherapy is to help the client employ the creativity and experience cycles. For instance, some clients need help in making use of either tightening or loosening their construing so as to employ them both in the creativity cycle. Experience cycles are core to the psychotherapy process and are seen as being conducted by the optimally functioning person over and over again. Likewise, the goals in therapy change again and again. 'Yesterday's useful insights become today's stubborn resistances and tomorrow's trivial clichés' (Kelly, 1980: 22). Another aspect of optimal functioning is that the person seldom has to resort to *being hostile* as the result of his experimental outcomes. He does not try to cook the books too often.

Thus, the goals of psychotherapy and the idea of the optimally functioning person are embedded in the notion that we are forms of motion. When we have problems, that motion becomes obstructed or slows down. The client who comes for psychotherapy is seen as being psychologically 'stuck'. The goal of therapy is to help him or her 'get on the move again'.

The Place of Personal History

Kelly states his position as being neither historical nor ahistorical. His fundamental postulate does not point to an exclusive commitment to either. He says:

> Historicalism is usually taken to mean that the course of events, once it is set in motion, elbows its way past the present and thrusts itself into the future. . . . That is not for me.
>
> [As for] ahistoricalism, the phenomenal present is a pretty small sample to work from, much too small, I'm afraid. So ahistoricalism, while emphasizing certain phenomenal points that stem from our postulate also, still tends to blot out parts of the record that we would have to consider important. Indeed, our model of man-the-scientist perhaps attributes a greater significance to the sweep of human history than does any other current psychological scheme. (Kelly, 1959b: 5–6)

In 'The psychology of optimal man', Kelly comes back to the theme of history and its relationship to phenomenology.

> The phenomenological psychologists, of whom I certainly am not one, usually take the view that it is only the experience of the passing instant that is of essential psychological significance. But I would argue that it is the whole story of mankind that is of greatest psychological significance. It is significant, not because it tells us what has happened to man, but because it tells us what has happened by the hand of man . . . (Kelly, 1980: 11)
>
> In psychotherapy particularly it makes a great deal of difference how the historical past is used. A therapist who is aware of the sweep of man's accomplishments, as well as what particular men have done about their handicaps, will envision the goals of his efforts quite differently from one who thinks in terms of disease entities, childhood traumata, or the closed economies of psychodynamic systems. As for the client, if he is one who regards his past as the successively emerging phases of his personal experience, each leading to a new outlook, he will make use of his therapeutic opportunities in a much different way than will one who recounts his past only to show what it has done to him and who looks at other men only to see who can tell him what to do. (Kelly, 1980: 24)

Thus, the personal construct psychotherapist neither feels the need to spend valuable time taking extensive notes of what has happened in the life of the client nor seeks 'the answer' in the client's past. The past is of value only if the client thinks it is or evidence emerges suggesting preverbal construing is preventing the client 'getting on the move again'.

Cross-Cultural Values

Kelly says psychotherapy 'should make one feel that he has come alive again'. This, as Beverly Walker points out, is an embedded value. However, the personal construct psychotherapist does not pre-determine what the client *should* become. There is no mould into which the unwary client must fit. However, there are, of course, embedded cultural values. For example, few therapists would allow their client to commit suicide or kill someone simply because this is what the client says they want to do. We all know that 'eating people is wrong'. But supposing we were to stretch the imagination and be doing psychotherapy with someone in a culture that practices cannibalism – what would we do? This is an extreme example, but raises the issue that there are embedded Western values in all our work. Therapists should be aware of them.

What can be said is that personal construct therapy is as value-free as it is possible to be. In *Counselling News* (1993), Amanda Webb discusses guide-lines for meeting the needs of Asian clients. These are to do with not imposing one's own social values on the client; listening to what the client actually says; showing respect for the client's values and so forth. These might have been written for a personal construct therapist. It is for this reason that some see it as an excellent approach for transcultural counselling and psychotherapy.

The Nature of Resistance

Personal construct theory dominates the practice of personal construct psychotherapy in all things. It therefore also leads to a particular approach to the psychotherapist's experience of the client's resistance in therapy. A person will resist changing for a number of reasons and the client is seen as being quite right to resist such change.

For instance, the client may be threatened by changes perceived to be imminent. He may see no meaning in the place towards which he is moving. This is often the case when the client is needing to change his core role construing. Here the need is to change essential aspects of himself. One client wrote a self-characterization about his need to resist such change, which included the following:

> He would like to change and yet remain himself
> He isn't sure that that wish isn't an irresolvable contradiction
> On the other hand to become someone else
> seems quite impossible even if it was desirable
> The changes that seem to be required seem so massive that it
> seems difficult to imagine how he could make those
> changes and still remain himself.

Perceptions of the enormity of change can lead to the client resisting change by becoming hostile in the sense of 'proving' they are right not to change. Kelly puts it this way:

> If the client is hostile he may, indeed, be making a whipping boy out of the therapist; but even this we feel is more profitably seen as an effort to

> retrieve some bad bets on which the client wagered more than he can afford. If the therapist has no more enlightened construction of what is going on than to insist that the client 'is being stubborn', it would seem that the therapist is hostile too. (Kelly, 1991, Vol. 2: 379)

On other occasions the change the client seeks is movement towards some ideal. Few people find the ideal attainable let alone liveable.

I have suggested that there are two types of change (Fransella, 1991). One is change *within the current system* and the other is change *to the system itself*. The examples given above are largely the latter. It is in these cases that clients are more likely to decide to persist with their current ways of relating to the world, however they may dislike those ways. For change to the system is likely to involve change to the very essence of 'the self'.

Kelly points out that the therapist can unknowingly create resistance by too much reassurance. Before getting a clear perspective of the client's construing system, part of the therapist's role is to create a good relationship with the client and part of that is to reassure the client. Many clients start out by making categorical statements about their problems: 'Nobody understands me.' The temptation for the therapist is to respond with something along the lines that it is unlikely that anyone can be understood one hundred per cent but that does not mean that people do not understand him in certain respects and regard him affectionately in these regards. It is possible, however, that the client is actually struggling to grasp the submerged opposite pole of the construct 'I don't understand people.' The therapist has successfully thwarted that attempt – at least for the time being.

Clients will always know their own construing system better than the therapist will. They are only seen as resisting what the therapist *thinks should be changing*. For the personal construct psychotherapist, clients are seen not as *resisting* change but rather as *choosing* not to change. Since the term 'resistance' has negative overtones, it is suggested that this be changed to the more positive term 'persistence'. So the question becomes: 'Why does my client persist in maintaining the *status quo*?'

A Suggested Distinction Between Counselling and Psychotherapy

Much has been written about the criteria that may be used to distinguish counselling from psychotherapy. This has often been in terms of length of treatment and psychological depth. There are also those who say that counselling applies to those 'normal' individuals looking for growth and psychotherapy as helping individuals who have some psychological dysfunction that prevents them leading 'normal' lives. Others say that it is not possible to identify criteria that distinguish between the two.

Personal construct theory provides some criteria that do distinguish between the two. One is that mentioned above. There are those who need to change aspects of themselves that are encompassed *within their present construing system* – this is counselling – and there are those who are going to need to *change the system itself* – this is psychotherapy. In theoretical terms, psychotherapy involves some reconstruing at a core role level whereas counselling does not seek to work in that area. Of course, counselling can inexorably move into psychotherapy and core role reconstruing and psychotherapy turn out to be counselling. But personal construct practitioners find this a useful rule-of-thumb distinction.

Another criterion that can be applied is the distinction between the construing *process*, which is psychotherapy, and the *content* of construing, which is counselling. For instance, if you are helping someone to tighten his construing and so prevent him from slipping into the chaos of loosened construing linked to the diagnosis of schizophrenic thought process disorder, you are practising psychotherapy.

Summary

So, what are the main contributions of personal construct theory and its philosophy to personal construct psychotherapy? What follows is not in order of importance. To produce a hierarchy of importance would deny the philosophical basis of personal construct psychology. Personal construct psychotherapists will have their own perceptions of what is important. This will depend on how each construes themselves in relation to the clients with whom they work. This means that nothing is – or should be – set in concrete. There should be no dogma of what personal construct psychotherapy *is*. The fact that the theory is described in such abstract terms gives each therapist great freedom. But each is also guided by personal construct theory in their understandings of the client and the relationship. Psychotherapy practice follows directly from the theory.

The client is the person with the knowledge about himself that, when identified, can bring about change. The therapist is only the catalyst. The client is stuck in a way of living and experiencing the world that is causing personal and often inter-personal distress. The client is empowered, being the acknowledged expert on his or her life. The essential difference here from the medical model is that the client is not someone to be 'worked on' but someone who finds their own key to their own liberation from their own jail.

Embedded in Kelly's description of one specific personal construct approach – fixed role therapy – is the idea both that we have created ourselves and can therefore re-create the person we now are, and that the self is someone to be taken seriously. It is something we can use our imaginations together on – client and therapist. This emphasis on the use of imagination, of working together, militates against a confrontational style. Humour also has a part to play.

Personal construct psychotherapy is an evolutionary process. Diagnosis is only ever based on hypotheses of how the client's construing is *now*, and looks at transitions. The client will change. So a new transitive diagnosis has to be devised and tested out by both therapist and client.

The personal construct psychotherapist's training places great emphasis on how to enter the phenomenal world of the client. There is the initial credulous listening – accepting and understanding the world as the client sees it. But the listening involves another skill: the therapist's ability to suspend, to put out of sight and mind, his or her own personal value-laden constructs. It is through the professional constructs that the personal construct psychotherapist filters the client's experiences. The therapist must also be able to subsume the client's world under these professional constructs in order to formulate each transitive diagnosis.

Kelly's personal construct psychotherapy provides an appropriately complex view of the client, as does psychoanalysis, but it is used in a way that ensures the process takes weeks or months rather than years. It deals with behaviour and cognitions as does cognitive behaviour therapy, but always in the additional context of the emotional and experiential aspects of the client's world.

All clients have a history and it is important how that history is construed. The client who sees his history as having determined his present problem will be very different from the client who sees his childhood trauma as part of his personal experience on his way through life.

Lastly, this model allows a very wide range of methods to be used. It is eclectic regarding techniques but the use of these techniques is very firmly theory-based. Some of these techniques and methods are covered in the next chapter.

3

Major Contributions to Practice

> A scientist's inventions assist him in two ways: they tell him what to expect and they help him see it when it happens. Those that tell him what to expect are theoretical inventions and those that enable him to observe outcomes are instrumental inventions. The two types are never wholly independent of each other, and they usually stem from the same assumptions. This is unavoidable. Moreover, without his inventions, both theoretical and instrumental, man would be both disoriented and blind. He would not know where to look *or* how to see. (Kelly, 1969i: 94)

Kelly used psychotherapy as the focus of convenience of his theory. But he also said that he used psychotherapy as an example of how his theory might be applied in general to human understanding.

My personal view is that Kelly made at least five major contributions to the practice of psychotherapy. First, he freed the psychotherapist from being confined to a specific set of methods and techniques. Second, he broke the stranglehold that traditional psychometrics had over assessment. He described what is now called 'repertory grid technique' as a way of studying the construing of an individual rather than comparing an individual's 'scores' with those of a standardized group of individuals. He showed how to quantify qualitative data.

Third, he developed methods of qualitative assessment, notably the 'self-characterization'. Fourth, he made the relationship between therapist and client one of partnership or equality. Lastly, he gave role play and enactment a central place in his therapy. From these he developed a specific method called 'fixed role therapy'. In addition, he provided many examples of the change process and how to facilitate it.

Freedom to Create the Tools for the Job

As already mentioned, one of the skills required of the personal construct psychotherapist is creativity. This means that the therapist is not tied to specific methods or specific tools. In this sense, personal construct psychotherapy is eclectic as far as techniques are concerned. Kelly says that personal construct psychotherapy

> does not limit itself to any pet psychotherapeutic technique. More than any other theory, it calls for an orchestration of many techniques according to the therapist's awareness of the variety and nature of the psychological processes by which man works toward his ends. (Kelly, 1980: 35)

Not being tied to specific methods or tools, the psychotherapist must be creative in choosing or developing the best ways of aiding reconstruction. In this sense the therapy is eclectic as far as techniques are concerned.

Breaking the Psychometric Stranglehold

The Place of Measurement in Psychotherapy

In Kelly's day, many humanistic psychologists did not like measurement or assessment. He did not agree. In his paper 'Humanistic methodology in psychological research' he says:

> It would, in my opinion, be a serious mistake for psychologists who hope to raise man from the position of an unwitting subject in an experiment to a posture of greater dignity, to abandon technology. The spirit of man is not enlarged by withholding his tools. . . . A man without instruments may look dignified enough to those who do not stand in his shoes, but he most certainly will be incapable of making the most of his potentialities. (Kelly, 1969g: 143)

It must never be forgotten that George Kelly trained first of all as a physicist and mathematician. He was therefore steeped in the ideas of measurement and had a real love of mathematics. What was so unusual was that he married theory, practice and measurement in his description of psychotherapy.

Just how important mathematics was to George Kelly can be seen from this comment he made to Denny Hinkle:

> Johann Herbart's work on education and particularly mathematical psychology influenced me. I think mathematics is the pure instance of construct functioning – the model of human behavior. (Hinkle, 1970: 91)

Kelly's delight in mathematics of course also spilled over into his choosing the scientist as his model of the person.

Dewey's influence on Kelly's thinking has already been mentioned in connection with the development of the theory of personal constructs. But there may be more to the Dewey influence than Kelly talks about. For Dewey, along with George Herbert

Mead (1863–1931), created the philosophy of *pragmatism*. They set out to show the advantages of applying scientific method to philosophy, psychology and sociology. Perhaps Kelly was drawn to the philosophy of pragmatism because it linked philosophy and a psychology of action with scientific method.

Nomothetic or Idiographic Measurement?

Psychometrics is about measuring an ability on one particular dimension – say, intelligence. A large sample of people complete a new test to establish 'norms' or 'normative data'. After that, the scores of one individual are tested against those norms to see how that individual performs *vis à vis* his or her peers. This comes under the heading of *nomothetic* measurement.

'Nomothesis' originally meant *law-giving*, and so now describes procedures or methods that are designed to discover general laws. Such psychometric tests are statistically-based and regarded as 'objective'.

The alternative is to try to gain an understanding of one individual. That comes under the name of *idiographic* measurement. 'Idio' comes from the Greek meaning 'own', 'personal', 'private' and is designed to study a person's own, personal, private 'signature'. Such methods are usually regarded as 'subjective' as their interpretation is left to the client or the therapist or both who look at the results through their own individual personal construct systems.

Kelly puts his case thus in relation to the psychology of personal constructs and the uses of measurement in the clinical setting:

> There are two ways in which one can look at psychological measurement and clinical diagnosis. On the one hand, he can seek to fix the position of the subject with respect to certain dimensions or coordinates – such as intelligence, extraversion, and so on – or to classify him as a clinical type – such as schizoid, neurotic, and the like. On the other hand, he can concern himself with the subject's freedom of movement, his potentialities, the resources which can be mobilized, and what is to become of him. From the point of view of the psychology of personal constructs, in which the emphasis is upon process rather than upon fixed position, the latter represents the more enlightened approach. Let us say, then, that the primary purpose of psychological measurement in the clinical setting is to survey the pathways along which the subject is free to move, and the primary purpose of clinical diagnosis is the plotting of the most feasible course of movement. As a whole, diagnosis may be described as the planning stage of therapy. (Kelly, 1991, Vol. 1: 141)

Kelly's espousing of the idiographic approach within the context of his commitment to establish a clinical psychology discipline with a scientific base must have been a risky business. Perhaps this, in part, accounts for his apparent ambivalence at having his 1955 work published.

Measuring Meaning for the Individual: The Repertory Grid

Assigning Numbers to Personal Constructs

First there was *the Rep Test.* That was Kelly's original method for inviting a person to provide their idiographic 'signature'. The focus was on eliciting some constructs about the roles the individual applies to people with whom they interact. Kelly suggested that twenty-four such role titles might provide a representative sample of those with whom the person relates. These would include members of the immediate family, such as 'mother'; non-family members such as boy or girl friends; an employer who is/was hard to get along with; a successful person the individual knows and so forth.

He described this Role Construct Repertory Test (or Rep Test) as 'a new diagnostic instrument which illustrates how our theoretical thinking can be applied to the practical needs of the psychotherapist' (Kelly, 1991, Vol. 1: 152).

One vital connection between theory and practice is the idea of the bi-polar nature of personal constructs. The place of this in the theory has already been discussed. If you say that a man is tall you do more than exclude all objects that are not tall. You are probably denying that the man is short. In daily living as well as in psychotherapy, we need to take into account just what it is the person feels he must negate. In practice, the opposite pole of the construct often provides considerable insight into the idiosyncratic meaning of that construct.

Another theoretical corollary of importance here is that of *range of applicability.* It is essential that all constructs come within the range of convenience of all the elements. All constructs must be able to be related to all the elements (the items, role titles and so forth, that are to be construed). For instance, one fairly common problem arises when people mix children with adults in their element selection. It may well be that a person would have difficulty in applying the construct *sexy–not sexy* to some if not all the child elements.

As far as it is possible to tell in advance, the elements should be a representative sample of the people in an individual's life. The use of role titles can ensure this by having the client include liked as well as not-liked people and so forth.

In Kelly's original Rep Test, constructs are elicited by presenting three of the role titles and asking in what important way two are alike but different from the third. Kelly gives eight different ways in which these triads of role titles can be compiled (see Kelly, 1991, Vol. 1: 155–60) but all focus on helping the person provide some of the personal constructs they used in dealings with others. From these elicited constructs, Kelly hoped the clinician might be able to derive hypotheses to aid the psychotherapy process.

But the physicist and mathematician appear again. Kelly was not content to rest his case here. He wanted to relate these personal constructs mathematically. To do this he invented his own form of the statistical procedure called factor analysis. It provides ways of seeing how '. . . constructs and figures are interwoven to give substance to the fabric of society' (Kelly, 1991, Vol. 1: 189). One of Kelly's major contributions to psychological practice generally and to psychotherapy practice in particular was thus to objectify subjective data.

Everything Kelly created is related to his theory of personal constructs – even factor analysis. The following comes under the heading 'The grasp of meaning'.

> Factor analysis can be regarded as a way of displaying information in an economical way. As we have suggested before, this is the answer to a minimax problem – how to reduce a maximum of information to a minimum of terms. It is the baffling complexity of psychological processes that makes psychologists seek to encompass a maximum of information, and it is the limited ability of the human mind to orient itself in hyperspace that makes them try to keep the number of factors at a minimum.
>
> But there is another problem, too. Man has difficulty construing along unfamiliar lines, even when they are drawn with mathematical simplicity. His notions are held fast in a network of personal constructs and any ideas or feelings that have not yet found their place in that network are likely to remain exasperatingly elusive. Science, therefore, not only has the task of coming to simple terms with events, but it also has the psychological task of achieving some accommodation between what man believes and what, indeed, confronts him. (Kelly, 1969j: 325–6)

Kelly's form of analysis for repertory grid data did not prove very popular. This was partly because of its complexity. But there also proved to be some mathematical difficulties with the tick/blank format which was used at the time. That is, the person was asked to say whether each construct did or did not apply to each of the people covered by the role titles. Bannister showed (1959) that misleadingly high correlations could be produced if there was great inequality between ticks and blanks on one element: for example, if one person in the grid was seen as an *unprincipled lecher* and one other person was seen as a *civil servant*. Now, it could be that the person completing the grid actually *did* see civil servants as being unprincipled lechers. But it is more likely that this was a correlation that appeared because there were so many blanks in the comparison.

Kelly had been aware of this problem and had described various ways in which such lopsided constructs could be eliminated. However, they did not satisfy Don Bannister, so he developed methods for overcoming this lopsidedness problem himself. From then on, there were several modifications of the grid format – the majority created by Bannister. At the present time, the most commonly used format is for the client to give ratings to the relationship he or she sees between any given construct and each element (see Fransella and Bannister, 1977, for details of the various forms of grid method).

Kelly saw the grid form of the Rep Test as a means of 'looking beyond the words'. One is able to study the interactions between the people (elements) in a grid and the constructs. For instance, is it only women who are seen as *affectionate* and only men as *reliable*? Or is there a pattern of relationships that indicates that 'being depressed' is a desirable thing to be because those who are 'not depressed' are *cold, hard and not liked*?

If you are going to use a grid to elicit data from your client, the way in which the client is prepared for this is important. In an analysis of some of George Kelly's therapy tapes, Bob Neimeyer gives us an example of how Kelly approached the matter with his client – Cal – who he had seen for five previous sessions:

> Maybe today is a good time to do something more formal and less involving and less tension provoking. You remember I mentioned we might do kind of a formal exercise to give me some better understanding of how you see things. I don't think you'll find this particularly threatening; if you do, by all means tell me. (Neimeyer, 1980: 85)

A principal feature of repertory grid technique is its extreme flexibility. It can be designed to investigate aspects of the construing of individuals or groups, and of thought content or thought process. It is important to realize that there is no *one* repertory grid. It is up to the individual psychotherapist to create their own according to the perceived needs of the client.

Concepts of Reliability and Validity

A further contribution to our understanding of the association between measurement and clinical practice concerns Kelly's approach to the psychometric concepts of reliability and validity of tests. It is not within the scope of this volume to look at the research that has been carried out in these areas as far as grids are concerned, but simply to indicate how Kelly has taken yet more concepts and modified them in relation to his own theoretical perspective.

Kelly's comment that *reliability* is a measure of a test's insensitivity to change was not facetious, but a logical deduction from personal construct theory. This sees the person as a form of motion and so a static mind is a contradiction in terms. Instead of expecting a measure to yield similar scores for the same subjects on different occasions (as is usual with nomothetic tests), we might do better to predict where stability and change, in a particular grid with a particular person at a particular time, are likely to occur.

Bannister (1962), for instance, used the correlation between two identical grids, one repeated immediately after the other (one way of testing the reliability of a measure), as a score to discriminate between the construing process of those identified as showing schizophrenic thought process disorder and the process of both psychiatric and non-psychiatric groups. Later developments of this approach yielded test–retest correlations for the non-psychiatric group of 0.80 and for the thought-disordered schizophrenic group of 0.18 (Bannister and Fransella, 1966). Those in the non-psychiatric group gave similar responses on the two occasions; those in the thought process disorder group did not.

Bannister argued that it seemed reasonable to regard reliability as itself an aspect of construing rather than solely as an entity which is either 'acceptable' or not in a particular instance.

As grid technique is not a single test and has no specific content, its *validity* can only be discussed in terms of whether it effectively reveals patterns and relationships in certain kinds of data. The grid is therefore very different from a questionnaire designed, for example, to measure aggression.

However, the validity of particular grids has been looked at, for instance, when designed as a nomothetic test such as the grid test of thought disorder (Bannister and Fransella, 1966) mentioned above. Validity can then be assessed in the traditional manner. Grids have also been used specifically to test their own validity. In 1967, Don Bannister and I sought to validate the results from a rank order form of grid to do with political parties against votes cast by the same people in a British general election. The ways in which people ranked those they knew in terms of *like I'd like to be* and *like me in character* were compared with the rankings of the same people (elements) on the constructs *likely to vote Conservative (Labour, Liberal)*. From these data, fairly accurate predictions could be made of how each person actually voted (Fransella and Bannister, 1967).

This is a good example of what Kelly meant when he described validity as 'the capacity of a test to tell us what we already know'.

Kelly specified five functions that should be fulfilled by any psychological method of measurement that is to be used in a clinical setting (Kelly, 1991, Vol. 1: 141–3):

1 It should 'define the client's problem in usable terms'. It is not enough to say it is 'valid'. It has to be 'valid' for something. 'Usability, rather than accuracy, per se, is the minimum standard for a good clinical test'.
2 It should 'reveal the pathways or channels along which the client is free to move'. For example, the most obvious way for one client to move was to abandon being *unbearable* and become *lovable.* Knowledge of these construct pathways can make unusual behaviour in a client understandable.
3 It should 'furnish clinical hypotheses which may subsequently be checked and put to use'. Kelly says: 'This is important! In the clinical setting it is not always necessary for the test to present the clinician with *conclusive* findings. Like any other psychological process, therapy proceeds by the successive application of hypotheses and the observation of their outcomes' (Kelly, 1991, Vol. 1: 142; italics mine).
4 It should 'reveal those resources of the client which might otherwise be overlooked by the therapist'. This means revealing what resources the client has mobilized or has available to mobilize to meet their problems.
5 It should 'reveal those problems of the client which might otherwise be overlooked by the therapist'. Kelly thought that clinicians sometimes get blinkered by their therapy. He thought it important for a test to show vulnerabilities of the client which the therapist cannot ignore.

Kelly equated validity with usefulness and saw understanding others as the most useful of activities. Thus, grid studies have sought to increase our understanding of individuals in many contexts including clinical, social relationships, linguistic meaning, children's construing, politics or sex. They have also been widely used in a nomothetic sense providing information about groups of individuals. The flexibility of the repertory grid is limited only by the inventiveness of those who use it.

Contrary to popular belief, a personal construct psychotherapist is not duty bound to use a repertory grid with a client. I suspect the majority of clients complete their psychotherapy never having seen a grid. Repertory grid technique is merely a method that *can* provide useful information on *some* occasions with *some* clients.

Assessment without Numbers

Grids have featured prominently as part of Kelly's work. But he describes two less well-known ways of eliciting the world-view of the client: the self-characterization and the life role.

The Self-Characterization

This was designed to fulfil Kelly's first principle: 'If you do not know what is wrong with someone, ask them, they may tell you' (Kelly, 1991, Vol. 1: 241). It is an example of the application of the *credulous approach* discussed in the previous chapter. One is not interested in the truth or falsehood of a person's views but simply in the ways in which they view themselves and their relationships with others. Its analysis does not rest on the derivation of quotients for pleasure–pain statements, or on counts of such things as negative and positive statements. Instead, as Kelly puts it, one 'listens to nature babbling to herself' and seeks to gain some insights into another's personal construct system.

The instructions for the self-characterization contain an invitation to 'tell' what is personally meaningful at the present time. Kelly suggests the following format:

> I want you to write a character sketch of (for example) Harry Brown just as if he were the principal character in a play. Write it as it might be written by a friend who knew him very *intimately* and very *sympathetically*, perhaps better than anyone ever really could know him. Be sure to write it in the third person. For example, start out by saying, 'Harry Brown is . . .' (Kelly, 1991, Vol. 1: 242)

The wording was worked out very carefully so as to give the person maximum room for manoeuvre. 'Sketch' is to suggest that general structure rather than elaborate detail should be written about. Emphasis on the third person is to indicate that it is not to be an account of faults or virtues, but rather of the person as a whole. Other phrases are designed to minimize threat implicit in any such activity and to enable the person to give speculations as well as facts.

One assumption built into the self-characterization is that the client will choose topics to talk about which have enough structure for him to make sense, but that he will also touch upon – however gingerly – areas in which he is uncertain.

The client's choice of topics also gives an indication of how he sees himself as distinguishable from others. If he thinks he is pretty ordinary in physical appearance, this is unlikely to be mentioned. Unless, of course, he is desperately concerned about being so ordinary – but that is likely to show up elsewhere.

Kelly suggests that the first sentence may usefully be looked at as if it were a statement of the person's general orientation to life now. The last sentence may give an indication of where the person sees themselves as going.

There are many ways of using the self-characterization in psychotherapy both as a method of assessment and as part of the therapeutic process. If particular areas of life are of interest then the wording of the instructions can be altered. Kelly gives an example of approaching retirement. A useful sketch is of the person before they became 'ill' followed by how they think they will be after their therapy. Or, at the start of therapy, the client can be asked to write two sketches, one of themselves as they are with their problem and one as they will be without the problem. It is quite clear that the writing of such character sketches provides insights for the client into his or her own construing as well as giving the therapist a clearer picture of the world in which the client lives. Some clients find writing a very powerful way of furthering the therapeutic process. I have described the use such a client made of the self-characterization format in my paper 'Nature babbling to herself' (Fransella, 1980).

Client's Construction of His or Her Life Role

This procedure, like all others described, is used in the context of the therapeutic process. There is no assessment for the sake of assessment in George Kelly's personal construct psychotherapy.

Questions to elicit the client's life-role structure may go along the following lines: 'What were some of your plans for the future when you were a child?' 'What did you want to be when you grew up?' 'What did you think it would be like to be a . . .?' 'What led you to change your mind?' 'What do you think about it now?' 'How did things go wrong?' And so forth.

The elicitation of the client's construction of his life role can serve many purposes. For instance, it might be used with a client who questions the purpose in his life. The aim is to show the client that there has been purpose and to suggest that there might still be purpose if he once finds it. It can also be particularly useful in the context of vocational or career counselling.

Equality in a Psychotherapeutic Relationship

We need to be careful here about the actual meaning of the word 'equal' in the context of a relationship between client and therapist. Kelly was contrasting the relationship with those in psychodynamic psychotherapy and in the behaviour therapies. In both these cases there is the assumption that the therapist has the knowledge and hopefully the answers to deal with the client's problems.

Kelly saw equality of relationship in terms of both partners having specialist knowledge and, with this specialist knowledge, being able to work together as a team. Clients know all about themselves, even if some of that knowledge is not readily available to them at the moment. The client can teach the therapist about this. The therapist has knowledge about some of the ways in which it is possible to help people find out more about themselves *and* ways of getting out of some of the psychological difficulties we can all find ourselves in from time to time. In that sense, the relationship is not one of equality. The psychotherapist in all therapies is the one who makes decisions about the best way to help the client move forward *at that particular time.*

Methods for Assisting the Psychotherapeutic Process

The Influence of Jacob Moreno

Kelly placed major emphasis on role play and enactment in psychotherapy. His interest in acting and the theatre has already been mentioned. For instance, as early as 1927 he was 'coaching in dramatics' at a junior college combined with the teaching of psychology and speech. It is therefore not surprising to learn that Jacob Moreno had an influence on Kelly's thinking. Moreno had developed the technique of *sociometry* to chart the group process and first published his journal – *Sociometry* – in 1937. Kelly used some of Moreno's sociometric ideas for his first Role Construct Repertory Test.

But Moreno had also been developing the therapeutic method of psychodrama in the 1930s along with group psychotherapy. At that same time, Kelly had been using enactment with his clients on a more or less ad hoc basis. He describes (1991, Vol. 1) how he had become aware of the lasting effect playing certain parts in drama can have on the actor. These and other observations made Kelly well able to understand what Moreno was doing with his psychodrama on a group basis.

Stewart and Barry (1991) discuss the influence of Moreno's ideas on Kelly. According to Barry's lecture notes taken in 1948, Kelly was particularly interested in Moreno's technique of spontaneous improvisation. Moreno (1937) explains that this 'stegreif' theatre lets people play any part they wish and that it is about being impromptu and 'warming up'.

According to Barry, Kelly had developed a form of group

improvisation in which 'people just decided in a general way the kind of people they'd portray, and go ahead and let the lines and plot take care of themselves – develop unplanned in front of the audience' (Barry, 1948). The focus of this method was to emphasize the social aspect of construing by having people enact someone other than themselves. This method has some links with Kelly's own fixed role therapy.

Fixed Role Therapy

In the form of fixed role therapy described by Kelly, the client is asked to become someone other than themselves for a period of about two weeks. One aim is to enable the client to see how it is possible to create a new person; not totally new, of course, but to see that it is indeed possible to change and to do it oneself. It was Kelly's indirect way of demonstrating his philosophy in action: how we need not be hemmed in by circumstances, how there are alternatives available for us to choose between.

This is by no means the be-all and end-all of personal construct psychotherapy. In fact, there are many who have never used the method in the all-embracing way in which Kelly describes it. It is worth spending time on as it personifies how personal construct theory applies to psychotherapy.

The client not only experiences behaving in different ways, but experiences how others respond to these differences. Some experiences turn out well while others would have been best not tried at all. But tried they were and lessons learned. Kelly says:

> Personal construct theory is not a cognitive theory, but a theory about how the human process flows, how it strives in new directions as well as in old, and how it may dare for the first time to reach into the depths of newly perceived dimensions of human life. . . . Man understands his world by finding out what he can do with it. And he understands himself in the same way – by finding out what he can make of himself, man is what he becomes. What he becomes is a product of what he undertakes – expected or by surprise. . . . [Here] . . . lies the ontological rationale of fixed role therapy. (Kelly, 1973: 5)

Briefly, the client writes a self-characterization. This is used by the therapist to prepare an *enactment sketch*. This is another self-characterization based on the first, but different in a number of important respects. The character in the sketch must appear to the client to be a possibility. It is to be an experiment for the client to enact this person – it is a scientific enterprise in which therapist and client are co-experimenters. The client finally accepts the sketch and agrees to play the role of this new person with a new name.

The enactment sketch is designed to develop a major theme

rather than changing specific concrete behaviours. For instance, if the client sees herself as *dependent* as opposed to *dominating*, the sketch might describe her as *interested in others*. The ways in which the new character is to behave in relation to these themes need to be well defined so that their limits can be clearly seen. The general aim is to set new processes in motion – get the client on the move – rather than to create a new person. The emphasis is on role perceptions. That is, the client is required to focus on how *others* are construing these new behaviours.

The person in the sketch is given a new name. It is important that the sketch describes someone who is both believable and acceptable to the client. When everyone is happy with the sketch, the client is asked to enact this new person for two or three weeks.

During the period of the fixed role enactment, the client has constant access to the therapist plus regular meetings at which the various experiments and their outcomes can be discussed.

It is hoped that the client will learn that much of the behaviour of others towards us is determined by our behaviour towards them. If we change our behaviour, so may others change theirs towards us. Another result of such an audacious experiment is the realization that we have invented ourselves – that we are not unalterable persons. Fixed role therapy is thus a model of the psychology and philosophy which underlies personal construct psychotherapy. The theory sees us as self-inventing; sees our behaviour as being our continuing experimentation; sees us as individuals who are enmeshed within a social context and who know ourselves through our experiences with others; and sees us as individuals whose exploration and change are essential aspects of life.

Kelly devotes over sixty pages to the carrying out of fixed role therapy. Anyone who feels they would like to learn more about it is directed to the original source (Kelly, 1991, Vol. 1: 268–334).

Enactment

Kelly also drew upon Moreno's self-presentation technique, in which the person plays himself or herself. This is what Kelly refers to as psychodrama. But both the spontaneous improvisation and the self-presentation methods aim to help the person change the way in which they see themselves. Implicit in all Kelly's modifications of Moreno's methods is the notion that each one of us is able to create and therefore re-create ourselves and also that such creation takes place in a social context.

Kelly preferred to use the term 'enactment' since it includes role play. With his special definition of role (construing the construction processes of others), the most involving type of enactment is role enactment. But enactment can take place without role involvement: although, as he says, the person soon starts to feel the need to understand the other's constructions.

What Kelly calls *casual enactment* within the therapy session serves a number of purposes. It helps the client elaborate their personal construct system, protects the client from involving core issues before he or she is ready to deal with them, and enables the client to see himself and his problems in perspective. Kelly likened the enactment procedures in psychotherapy to projective procedures in psychodiagnosis.

An example of casual enactment in therapy is given in Neimeyer's study of a taped interview by George Kelly with a client (Neimeyer, 1980). The session did not quite go as the therapist planned.

> *K*: If you were to . . . imagine yourself in my place, and I were asked to describe Cal Weston to someone, with some care, what do you imagine you would say? You're Dr. Kelly, describing Cal Weston to a close associate in whom you have confidence, and you wish to sketch accurately and with some depth, some sensitivity, the Cal Weston that has been seen for eleven interviews now . . . I'll be the friend; you're Dr. Kelly.
> *C*: Outside of what I've said, I don't know if I could say anything; I can't think of anything.
> *K*: 'I'm seeing a fellow by the name of Cal Weston'. This could be your first sentence. Now what sentence comes next?
> *C*: (Long pause)
> *K*: What kind of a patient is this, Dr. Kelly?
> *C*: I'm trying to think of something, but I'm not getting anywhere fast.
> *K*: You mean you can't describe him, Dr. Kelly? (Long pause.) How well do you think you know your patient, Dr. Kelly?
> *C*: I don't know how that would be answered. I'm just drawing a blank in my mind, that's all. Nothing.

Neimeyer sees this as a good example of casual enactment in that it occurred spontaneously during the therapy session. Kelly demonstrates in this enactment how he drops in and out of role. For instance, he was aware of Cal's difficulties with role construing – that is, seeing things from another person's point of view. Cal has difficulty with this and tries to 'not play the game'. Kelly deals with this by staying in role himself and even interprets Cal's silences as if he were 'Kelly'. Unfortunately, this tactic does not work, so Kelly drops the role to discuss Cal's anxieties.

> *K*: How do you feel about this kind of exercise? Is it disturbing?
> *C*: *No*. I just get nothing.
> *K*: Do you have some doubt about how I would really describe you?
> *C*: I don't know how you would describe me . . . to make a description,

I'd have to remember what I've talked to you about in the past . . . and I can't remember anything . . . the only thing that I've been able to construct so far is that I came in to see you, and, uh, felt I had a problem when I came in, logically enough. But the development beyond this is zero.

K: What did this fellow talk about, Dr. Kelly?

C: (Pause) Well, for one thing, whenever you mention me as Dr. Kelly, I get an uneasy feeling. I don't like it. But to carry on with the idea . . .

K: Well, we can change this. Go on . . .

C: I'd say one of the problems was the problem in school, not being able to achieve and maintain a standard which the individual feels he should.

K: Um-hm. This was his main, or his initial comment?

C: Yeah. The discussion was about the individual and his problems in school, and family background, educational background. (Pause) . . .

In resuming the enactment, Kelly becomes more concrete and simply asks Cal as 'Kelly' to recall some of what had been discussed in the previous sessions. This tactic meets with some success, but Cal soon dries up again. Kelly then modifies the role play so as to make it less anxiety-provoking.

K: Well, let's say that you're Dr. Jones, who has been seeing Cal Weston. Does that make it a little easier? It takes some of the 'personal' out of it.

C: Yeah, but still there's an uneasiness in that you're asking me to make a judgment which I'm not qualified to make . . .

They then discuss Cal's concern about making a judgement that would not represent a 'true picture' of what has transpired from the therapist's point of view. Before giving up the task entirely, Kelly has one more try at staying in role.

K: May I ask one more question of you in your role as Dr. Jones? Dr. Jones, what kind of *person* do you think this man is?

C: What do you mean?

K: What motivates him? Or let me put it this way – what is it like to meet him? What kind of *feeling* do you get when you meet him?

C: I doubt that I could answer that.

K: Is it a little threatening to ask this question?

C: I don't think so (loudly): I just don't see how I can reflect on myself and describe myself from that sort of view.

Cal goes on to explain the difficulty he encounters in taking Kelly's perspective.

C: I'd have to . . . guess at how someone else might see me. But I would have no idea, no basis for describing the person that was doing the seeing, or how he would see me.

K: Do you feel that you have no basis for knowing how I see you, or do you have a *sense* of how I see you?
C: I'd never thought of it. I think if anything, I tried to keep an idea like that out.
K: Why?
C: Well . . . what I expect of you is an objective, rational study of my problems, provided you can find them, the roots of them, and trying to help me sort them out through questions and discussions. At least that's what I assume . . . the role of the psychologist is. What was the question again? (Laughs).
K: What kind of a *sense*, what kind of an *impression*, what kind of *feelings* do you think I have about you? Or did you have the feeling, or the conviction that I would have as few feelings as possible and be as analytic as possible?
C: *And* the development of any emotional friendship with you would tend to lead me to answer any questions . . . with a bias towards maintaining that friendship . . . I'm not in a position (to play your role). I would be assuming some of the points of view you might have, and to develop those points of view I'd have to come to know you a little bit, and know how you think and how you feel. I've tried to prevent anything like that from happening, so that I wouldn't feel emotionally involved in our personal relationship. That's strictly – professional. You're the doctor. I'm going to keep this strictly on an 'M.D./guy with a cut throat' situation.
K: What kind of situation?
C: 'Cut throat'. I tried to come up with something rather radical.

After this in-depth exploration of the nature of Cal's resistance to the enactment, Kelly has a clear understanding of how Cal construes his therapy and the role he expects the therapist to play. As he frequently does, Kelly checks on his interpretation of the client's viewpoint before moving on.

K: This discussion we're having now is good. Now let me see if I understand. This is my examination now; you see if I can pass it. In a sense you are saying, 'I'm going to keep Kelly at arm's length, so that he'll be a kind of doctor, so that he can cut my throat if it's logically required. I'll keep him at a distance so that I can tell him the worst about me, so that I can bare myself to the worst that can happen. For if I get too close, I'll be afraid of losing him, and I'll start having a kind of personal relationship.

Having identified why Cal has been having so much difficulty in stepping into his therapist's shoes, Kelly picks up a theme that has been running through all the interviews, which is to do with *being rational* versus *being emotional*. Kelly offers an interpretation to Cal of how he sees this theme.

K: I think I get more of a sense of how you feel. It isn't that you don't want to go into this uncharted [emotional] area, but you want to make sure that when you do go in that you don't flounder, that you don't become lost, that you can still relate it to something that you do know, that you do consider firm on the outside, back in the realm of rationality.

C: Yeah. I don't want to go into this thing and then be at a complete loss as to what we've covered, to have you play back the record or something so that I can understand what's happened.

K: So you're saying essentially . . . 'For God's sake, don't throw me into chaos all at once!'

C: Yeah, yeah, yeah! That's it! I hadn't thought of it from that point of view but it fits; it fits what I've said very clearly.

Group Psychotherapy

Little reported on, but clearly described by Kelly, is his approach to group psychotherapy. He saw group therapy as often being the therapeutic context of choice, as with severely disturbed clients in a hospital setting; if not the therapy of choice, then to be used in conjunction with individual therapy.

Since the broad aim of personal construct psychotherapy is to help the person become more effective in anticipating others and himself, then the group setting provides a broader base for experimenting with new ways of construing others and for trying out new roles. Those in individual therapy have to conduct most of their experimentation and try out their new roles in the potentially hazardous 'outside world', whereas in group therapy the individual has the protective walls of the therapy setting. As Kelly says, 'it is like having a large, well-equipped laboratory with a variety of figures in it, in contrast to a small laboratory with only one figure in it' (1991, Vol. 2: 418). The differences in the personalities of the group members give the individual the opportunity of developing a more comprehensive role for himself. In theoretical terms, this means the individual is likely to get a variety of evidence to validate (or invalidate) his particular behavioural experiments.

Negative evidence is more likely to occur in group than in individual psychotherapy and it would be counter-productive to allow a client who has problems with feeling a failure and so forth to be confronted with evidence that validates those feelings. Kelly's view is that many therapists are reluctant to venture into group psychotherapy because of this fear of invalidation for the client. However, if the group is being conducted along the lines he proposes, such negative evidence for an individual client would be taken care of.

He makes two other points about the advantages of group therapy. One concerns dependency and the other is to do with stereotyping.

As was discussed in the previous chapter, Kelly sees all of us as being dependent on others to some extent. The issue is whether or not an individual is able to disperse his or her dependencies among others. To put all your dependencies in one basket is not a good idea for the obvious reason that if, for whatever reason, that person should stop being around, you have no one else on whom to depend – except yourself. For Kelly, the first stage of the group process is the encouragement of the members to disperse their dependencies amongst the group rather than having each client dependent on the therapist – as is the case, for instance, in group analytical therapy. He points out that this can be threatening to some therapists who have to learn to see clients' independence from him or her as a positive event.

Cassie Cooper, who had trained as a Kleinian analyst and in group analysis, reported her reactions to this group independence (Cooper, 1982). On one occasion she had to do the unforgivable in analytic terms – leave the room during a session. Her anticipations of what would confront her when she re-entered the therapy room were totally invalidated. Group members had done two things. They had changed the seating arrangements and turned on a light, and they were in such deep discussion together that they did not appear to notice that the therapist had re-entered the room. Kelly would have approved. So did Cassie Cooper, on reflection.

One of the most important advantages of the group setting is the opportunity it provides for clients to divest themselves of pre-emptive construing and its mate, constellatory or stereotypical construing. Pre-emptive constructs are those that say 'My mother is my mother and *nothing but* my mother'. In the group setting the client has experience of how other people view 'my mother'. There will be the opportunity to explore the possibility that 'my mother' can be construed in a number of other ways as well. A different type of rigidity is constellatory construing. This is to do with, for instance, seeing everyone who cannot control their weight as weak-willed, weepy and vain. The group may well provide evidence that such a person is far more complex than this stereotype implies.

Kelly suggested that the group process evolves through six stages. The first stage is *the initiation of mutual acceptance and support.* Here *acceptance* is defined in role terms – that is, the readiness to see the world through another's eyes. In the group situation, support rests on acceptance. There must be at least one person with whom each client can safely conduct experiments knowing there will be an attempt to understand what the experiments are about.

The essential feature of this stage is that the therapist must never allow any member to put themselves in a vulnerable position until it is clear that at least some members of the group will support that person. There are many ways of encouraging the development of support, such as enactment or role play, care being taken that none of the situations played should be too near the personal biography of any one member.

Next comes the *initiation of primary role relationships*. Again, the term 'role' is used in the Kellyian sense of standing in the other's shoes and trying to look at the world through that other's eyes. Kelly suggests using the last enactment that has been performed. Members are asked to talk about what the performer might have been experiencing during the enactment.

The third phase of the group therapy process is the *initiation of mutual primary enterprises*. The members of the group now start to take charge. They are beginning to suggest what the group might explore next or try to discover the answer to a particular problem. They are encouraged to propose behavioural experiments for themselves and others.

The group turns to the *exploration of personal problems* in the fourth stage of therapy. These personal problems are those that have their focus outside the group. If enactment is used, members now enact situations from their own and each other's lives. Kelly points out how this is similar to yet different from the psychodrama proposed by Moreno and his colleagues.

> We would agree with them that there is validation or 'reality testing' involved. However, we would place somewhat greater emphasis upon the value of the experience to the person who serves as an 'auxiliary ego'. It reestablishes him in a role relationship, a fact which should help him deal with his own guilt feelings. It shows him how a team approach can be used to solve personal problems. It helps him place his own problems in a social frame of reference by observing their similarity to the problems that other persons have. (Kelly, 1991, Vol. 2: 429)

Now we come to the fifth phase of personal construct group therapy which is to do with the *exploration of secondary roles*. The members are starting to interpret events from the points of view of those outside the group. This is the stage in which members are encouraged to extend the lessons they have learned within the group to those in the world outside and to humanity at large. Kelly advocates the use of sociodrama here. This focuses on social situations rather than personal problems which are the focus of psychodrama. In sociodrama, the person is extending his construing of himself and other individuals to the construing of himself in relation to society as a whole.

The sixth and last phase begins when a member tells the group he is involved in ventures outside the group. The group now only acts as a support and an insurance policy against the failure of this venture. As the outside becomes more and more of a focus for members, so the group is moving itself to its completion.

Methods for Assisting the Process of Reconstruction

Apart from methods for helping the psychotherapeutic process, Kelly detailed eight main ways in which construing can change. But it is important always to bear in mind that, with personal construct psychotherapy and most other therapies, nothing takes place in a vacuum. All the time the therapist is alert to the emotional state of the client, to the threats there may be in what the client is being asked to do, of the issues likely to raise anxiety and those likely to stop the change process dead in its tracks as the client becomes hostile in order to protect themselves.

Kelly puts these change strategies in the context of everyday life, saying that 'these are the same ways that, on one kind of occasion or another, man has always employed in dealing with perplexities' (Kelly, 1969d: 231). The following are seen in the context of the client and therapist working as a team.

Slot-Change

The first is to reverse the client's position on one major construct axis. 'Call this slot-rattling, if you please' (Kelly, 1969d: 231). Such slot-change is often regarded as rather superficial change. The client moves from being *subservient* to being *dominating*. This may well have been tried before, with sometimes disastrous consequences. But with the help of the therapist, the client may be able to see some of the advantages of being *dominant* and some of the behaviours that make their *dominance* unacceptable to others or in certain contexts. All too often, however, it becomes a see-saw. The client feels dominant when confident and subservient when feeling low.

Shift-Change

The second is also inclined to be superficial change. 'They can select another construct from the client's ready repertory and apply it to matters in hand' (Kelly, 1969d: 231). But with care, this can be used to advantage. In the example above, the client might come to see that *being listened to* as opposed to *doing the listening* is an alternative way of looking at the situation. Such shift-change may not appear great at the time, but, since the theory states that constructs are hierarchically organized into a system, all reconstructions can have ramifications within the system that are not apparent on the surface.

Verbalize the Preverbal

The third type of reconstruction is to 'make more explicit those preverbal constructs by which all of us order our lives in considerable degree' (Kelly, 1969d: 231). This is a strategy almost inevitably used in psychotherapy. Construing at a low level of awareness produces behaviour and feelings that are little if at all understood. With some clients this is the central cause of their current problems. Verbalizing the preverbal is not easy and usually takes some time.

Controlled Elaboration

The fourth method is to 'elaborate the construct system to test it for internal consistency' (Kelly, 1969d: 231) by *controlled elaboration*. The constructs are not necessarily revised, but they are explored and defined more clearly. For instance, a person who sees himself as *gentle* on a *gentle–aggressive* dimension is helped to spell out what being *gentle* actually means and what behaviours go with it. He may come to the realization that a person can be both but in different situations. He thus learns more about his own construing system which makes it more workable for him.

Predictive Validity and Range of Convenience

The fifth involves testing constructs for their predictive validity and the sixth increasing or decreasing the range of convenience of certain constructs by making them apply to more events. Both are quite straightforward and rarely involve any complex therapist–client interaction.

Rotating Existing Reference Axes and Creating New Ones

The seventh and eighth involve creativity. That is, they involve the client in first loosening their construction – by the use of fantasy, reporting dreams, free association, or relaxation – and then tightening their construing to complete the creativity cycle. Kelly describes these strategies as 'altering the meaning of certain constructs; rotating the reference axes' and 'erecting new reference axes. This is the most ambitious undertaking of all' (Kelly, 1969d: 231).

The Personal Construct Approach to Some Specific Behaviours

Since Kelly's theory is about the total human being, it is not surprising that he had things to say about specific behaviours. Perhaps the two best to exemplify this are dreaming and weeping.

Dreaming

Theoretically, dreaming is seen as a supreme example of loose construing. The tale keeps shifting: what was seen one way one minute is seen differently the next. Dreaming typically involves construing at a low level of awareness – often preverbal construing. Dreams can be related to submerged poles of constructs also. The therapist is advised to look at the construct as a bi-polar entity and not to be concretistic. Kelly cites a client whose therapist is short and fat and who dreams of a tall thin man who tempts him into doing wicked things. Rather than think what tall, thin and wickedness may mean to the client, Kelly suggests the therapist think along the constructs *tall–short*, *thin–fat*, and *wickedness–goodness*. If he looks carefully, he may see that one of the elements sitting along these constructs is himself.

Kelly parts company with the psychoanalysts concerning the interpretation of dreams. As one might expect, he thinks the client is the only person who can interpret what has been experienced. He explains that the interpretation of dreams in terms of symbolism is assuming that the therapist's meaning for the symbol will also be that of the client. From Kelly's standpoint, that is an assumption that just cannot be made.

One of the three types of dreams Kelly identifies is the *gift dream*. These he thinks occur when the client has come to understand the symbolic meanings the therapist imposes on different aspects of the dream. The client then comes to dream in symbolic terms. Not much therapeutic progress will be made here. 'The client is amusing himself with the infantile constructs which the therapist has helped him name and manipulate verbally' (Kelly, 1991, Vol. 2: 338).

Clients are said to learn the language of their therapists. Clients having Freudian psychoanalysis have Freudian dreams, those in Jungian analysis have Jungian dreams. I do not know if clients having personal construct therapy have Kellyian dreams, but I am sure that we attempt to get our clients to view the world 'as if' there were alternative ways of looking at things. For how else are they ever to move on? They do not have to see their present ways as 'wrong' but simply accept that it may be useful to explore some alternatives. One can but speculate on what 'gift' the client might bring to a personal construct psychotherapist.

The personal construct psychotherapist does not interpret dreams, but leaves that to the client. That does not mean that interpretations may not be given in personal construct psychotherapy. As has been discussed in the previous chapter, interpretation is more along the lines of encouraging the person to come to their own conclusions by tentative suggestions like 'It occurs to me that . . .'; 'That reminds me of something you said the other day . . .'

Then there are *mile-post* dreams. These may assume epic proportions, are vivid and may contain elements of other dreams. They are vivid and unlike other dreams because they are tightly construed. Kelly says that his experience and theory lead him to see these as likely to indicate a major transition in the construction system of the client. 'It is our belief that a therapist should be prepared to enter a new phase of treatment whenever such a dream is reported' (Kelly, 1991, Vol. 2: 339).

Lastly, there are the usual type of *preverbal* dreams. These are vague, jumbled, contain no conversation: the sorts of dream we all experience and usually refer to when talking about dreaming. Kelly's example shows how he constantly uses the professional constructs to give meaning to an event.

> She was not sure she had dreamt at all. She had a vague feeling that she was lying in a crib, that she was feeling isolated from a man and a woman who were in the room. It seemed as though there were a netting between herself and the woman. The woman seemed like a certain aunt who was pretty and to whom she was much attracted when she was a very young child. The man seemed like an uncle whom she remembered as the first person in her life who had seemed to accept her. The most important feature of the setting appeared to be the netting, which seemed to excommunicate her from the persons with whom she had sought or had found a role relationship.
>
> The dream was reported in fragments and the client had the feeling that some of it might have been a memory, a story that she had been told, an old fantasy, or even something which she might be making up on the spot. It was definitely associated with feelings of unworthiness and guilt; indeed, the feeling of loss of role was the principal feature of the dream. This dream, together with other features of the case, established the deep-seated and preverbal nature of the client's guilt feelings as an important fact to be considered by the therapist. Moreover, it throws light upon one of the client's own aggressive techniques, that of excommunicating other people from her own society. This technique had been her principal second line of defence and accounted for many of the constricting measures which she employed. (Kelly, 1991, Vol. 2: 340–1)

Weeping

Kelly spends quite a time (1991, Vol. 2: 387–91) talking about crying, and links it, in nearly all cases, to anxiety. That is, it most likely occurs in someone who is finding their ways of construing the world inadequate for dealing with the current situation. But the converse cannot be assumed. The person who does not cry but sits in silence cannot be assumed to be without a high level of anxiety. As evidence of his interest in the subject, Kelly describes ten types of weeping! A story is told of him that, with his acting ability, he would demonstrate some of the types of weeping to his psychotherapy students and would shed real tears.

Diffuse-inarticulate weeping is the purest expression of anxiety. The person finds it impossible to stop no matter what the topic. Often they are unable to say exactly what it is they are crying about. Kelly regards this as a danger sign. It may indicate that the client is near psychological collapse and is a potential suicide risk.

Infantile weeping 'has an animal-like whimpering quality about it'. This is seen in clients with brain lesions and is sometimes called 'the organic cry'. If the client exhibits this type of crying, Kelly says a neurological examination is called for.

Regressive weeping is, as its name suggests, accompanied by child-like behaviours. It suggests that the client may be willing to relate to the therapist in the role of an infant. The therapist may decide to accept this preverbal role relationship to start with so that something can be built from it.

Loose weeping relates to the client whose behaviour seems to be inappropriate to the ideas expressed. This is commonly seen in acute schizophrenia. It is worth noting here that Kelly believed that the psychotherapist can sometimes be of help to those diagnosed as suffering from schizophrenia.

Situational weeping relates to a specific event which causes a loss of structure. As soon as the situation is over, structure returns and the client ceases crying. 'If the therapist is sure that this is the type of weeping that he has on his hands, the therapist need not feel that he has to stop it.' The client will do so of his own accord. 'Moreover, the therapist may wish to use the situational anxiety to get the client down to business.'

What Kelly calls *histrionic weeping* relates to that problem that has almost disappeared – hysteria. This type of crying is betrayed by its acting quality. 'If he is clever, he may enact the part of a martyr.' Kelly sees little disadvantage to this type of crying except that it gets in the way of the therapy.

The client weeps in a *hostile* way to prove the therapist is no good. This client will make sure that his crying is loud enough to carry outside the consulting room. 'The client cries in such a manner as to make it clear that he is being misunderstood and abused by his therapist.'

In *constrictive weeping* the client withdraws more and more into himself. He feels guilty about everything, and nothing is worthwhile or safe. The weeping becomes worse and worse. It is seen most often in those who are severely depressed. It should not be allowed to continue as the client may become exhausted. There is also a danger of suicide here.

Agitated weeping is an encouraging sign to the therapist and is seen as a form of aggression (active elaboration of one's perceptual field) on the part of the client. There is bodily movement as the anxiety is not so great as to paralyse the client.

Lastly, there is *façade weeping* which Kelly describes as one of the most interesting types from the point of view of those in a counselling situation with less seriously disturbed clients. It is similar to histrionic and hostile weeping except that the function is different. It is seen as an attempt to persuade the therapist and the client himself 'that he has a real problem'. Kelly sees the crying as a façade, designed to magnify problems in one area to prevent exploration in another area where there is real cause for concern.

Façade anxiety may be suspected in the client who is too specific about his or her problem. Or one who continually moves the interview into an impasse. One way of dealing with this is to challenge the façade and say it does not make sense and that little useful can be accomplished until the client is ready to talk about the 'real' problem.

Summary

This chapter is about how Kelly put his theory to work. The foundations of everything in the chapter have been laid in Chapter 2, because personal construct psychotherapy is personal construct theory and philosophy in action.

Kelly's description of fixed role therapy was essentially the essence of personal construct theory given the breath of life. This, plus his emphasis on enactment and role play, focuses attention on one of the corner-stones of personal construct theory – that all behaviour is (or can be viewed as) an experiment. Although much useful experimentation takes place within a session, the vast majority takes place between sessions. The emphasis has thus shifted from the importance of the therapist–client relationship to the client and the outside world. It is there that the experiments designed in the consulting room get tested out. The client is very much in charge of her own creation.

Apart from fixed role therapy, he gave an original account of the process of group psychotherapy and went as far as to say that it was his method of choice.

Kelly made three contributions concerning measurement and assessment in relation to psychotherapy. He showed how it was possible to quantify aspects of an individual client's world rather than having to resort to such tools as 'personality tests'; he demonstrated that methods of 'assessment' did not *have* to include numbers; and he developed a method that enables the psychotherapist to 'get beyond the words' of the client.

Although he did make some practical contributions to psychotherapy in the way of methods and procedures, perhaps one of his major contributions was the freeing of the therapist from being tied to specific methods and techniques. The way the therapist behaves and the tools she uses are dictated by personal construct theory, her transitive diagnoses of the client's problems and her own ingenuity.

4
Criticisms and Rebuttals

The Issues

Criticisms of personal construct theory have been slow in coming. The main reason for this must surely be its enormous breadth of coverage and, thereby, its complexity. To be truly critical of something you have to have a depth of understanding.

The selection of criticisms to cover is, like everything else, subject to the construing of such issues by the author. It is therefore I who have chosen the topics and they are ones I believe to be major. Others may obviously have different views.

It seems reasonable to start with Kelly's own view that the value of a theory lies in its usefulness and, once that usefulness fades, so should the theory. There is then the issue of whether he did enough to convince us that emotions and feelings are part of the construing process or whether personal construct theory is just a cognitive theory. Both are centrally to do with the mind–body controversy and the question of whether Kelly was successful in arguing that we could usefully do without that construct.

There is then the often-expressed issue of the extent to which Kelly gave adequate attention to the effects of the social context within which we all exist. That is followed by a discussion of why Kelly did not include any theoretical statements about the processes of child development. Lastly, there is the rather new topic of constructivism and what is happening in the field of psychotherapy as more and more people see themselves as 'constructivists'.

There have also been criticisms of the ways in which repertory grid technique has been developed. But these are of such a specialized nature that they find no place in this volume on Kelly's contributions to psychotherapy. Suffice it to say that repertory grid technique is alive and well as a methodology and is widely used in many contexts, including psychotherapy.

The Usefulness of Personal Construct Theory

Apart from dying because of the validity of criticisms levelled against it or massive research evidence invalidating it, a theory will also be replaced when it has ceased to be found useful. Kelly sowed the seeds of the replacement of his own theory at some future date in the following way:

> A theory provides a basis for an active approach to life, not merely a comfortable armchair from which to contemplate its vicissitudes with detached complaisance. Mankind need not be a throng of stony-faced spectators witnessing the pageant of creation. Men can play active roles in the shaping of events. How they can be free to do this and still themselves be construed as lawful beings is a basic issue in any psychological theory.
>
> The answer lies, first of all, in our recognition of the essentially active nature of our universe. The world is not an abandoned monument. It is an event of tremendous proportions, the conclusion of which is not yet apparent. The theories that men employ to construe this event are themselves incidents in the mammoth procession. The truths the theories attempt to fix are successive approximations to the larger scheme of things which slowly they help to unfold. Thus a theory is a tentative expression of what man has seen as a regular pattern in the surging events of life. But the theory, being itself an event, can in turn be subsumed by another theory, or by a superordinate part of itself, and that in turn can be subsumed by another. A theory is thus bound only by the construction system of which it is understood to be a part – *and, of course, the binding is only temporary, lasting only as long as that particular superordinate system is employed.* (Kelly, 1991, Vol. 1: 14; italics mine)

Its Approach to Emotions and Feelings

The statement that Kelly deals inadequately with emotions and feelings refuses to lie down and die. Although Kelly's theory explicitly states that construing involves both thinking and feeling, as discussed in Chapter 2, it will be dealt with here in more depth to show what the whole argument seems to be about.

It was Jerome Bruner, the Harvard University Professor of Psychology, who in 1956 opened the debate about Kelly not dealing adequately with the 'emotions'. He starts out by saying:

> These excellent, original, and infuriatingly prolix two volumes easily nominate themselves for the distinction of being the single greatest contribution of the past decade to the theory of personality functioning. Professor Kelly has written a major work. . . . Where does the book succeed and where fall down? . . . The book succeeds, I think, in raising to a proper level of dignity and importance the press that man feels

> toward cognitive control of the world. It succeeds too in recognizing the individuality and 'alternativeness' of the routes to mental health. It succeeds in providing a diagnostic device strikingly in keeping with its presuppositions.
>
> The book fails signally, I think, in dealing convincingly with the human passions. (Bruner, 1956: 355)

Also in the same journal, Carl Rogers (1956) wrote a review of Kelly's work under the heading 'Intellectualized psychotherapy'. Similar criticisms have continued over the ensuing forty years. Some, like Mackay, take it to extremes by saying 'PCT has been widely criticised on the grounds that it is too mentalistic. The ideal rational man, as depicted by Kelly and Bannister, seems more like a counter-programmed robot than a human being who is capable of intense emotional experience' (1975: 128). In the same year we have Peck and Whitlow saying:

> Kelly's approach to emotion is deliberately psychological but in order to achieve this position he is forced to ignore a wealth of knowledge from the field of physiology; furthermore some of the definitions seem to fly in the face of common sense. Bannister and Mair (1968, p. 33) state that 'Within this scheme "emotions" lose much of their mystery'; it can be argued that they also lose most of their meaning. (Peck and Whitlow, 1975)

Kelly became concerned about this issue quite early on. He realized that he had not succeeded in putting over his point about emotions being related to our awareness of our own construing. He spells out this need for elaboration in an interview. He had been talking about the writing of books and how he sees himself as writing several books at a time:

> but none of those gets written. And those that do get written are unlikely ever to be published. I was counting up the other day and I believe of five books I have written only one has been published and that, I think, was a mistake. Ah, well! Was I telling you about this business of the human feeling? Well, after the book that was published, was published, a good many people referred to construct theory as a cognitive theory. So I listened to this for several years and decided that something should be done about it. So I cooked up the idea of writing a book – perhaps not even identifying it as a 'psychology' book – a tentative title of which was to be *The Human Feeling*. Of course, I had once suggested we shouldn't use the term 'feeling'. But there is no reason why you shouldn't use it as the title of a book since the titles of books never have to be accounted for by the books. Anyway, I started to write this and then I gave a talk at Harvard in the Spring of 1959, after which Gordon Allport told the students that my theory was not really a cognitive theory but an 'emotional' theory. Later on the same afternoon, Harry Murray came up to me and said, 'You know you are an existentialist, don't you?' I think at the time I had heard the word existentialism or something of the sort.

> But this set me to try to find out what it was that I was. Anyway, the book on *The Human Feeling* has not been completed. (Kelly, 1966)

The chapters that he wrote for 'The Human Feeling' were collected together by Brendan Maher and published in 1969. Great use has been made of them in this volume to help spell out Kelly's views.

The holistic nature of the personal construct theory view of the person has important implications for psychotherapy as well as for our understanding of ourselves and others. For Kelly, to perceive of the person as being divided into segments such as emotion (affective) and thinking (cognitive) not only does the person an injustice, but impedes our approach to understanding.

Kelly integrated emotional experiences within his theory by seeing them as relating to an awareness that our construing system is in a state of transition or an awareness that it is inadequate for construing the events with which we are confronted. We 'feel' when we are aware that our system for construing the events milling around us is inadequate or seriously lacking or is about to change in some very radical way. Experiencing and construing are part and parcel of the same process. We can no more construe without experiencing than we can experience without construing.

As has already been pointed out, construing does not have to be in words. The person who is in deep meditation with no words in his world of experience, is still actively construing. But he is using another subsystem. This is the subsystem with which he makes contact with this other world of experience. The person absorbed in a piece of music is very actively construing – it would have no sense otherwise – and yet that person is unlikely to be having logical arguments going around in her head. Construing *includes* feeling.

By incorporating emotional experience into the process of construing, Kelly neatly side-stepped the complex issue of whether what I call anxiety is the same as what you call anxiety. We tend to use the word in the same situations and so have some understanding of each other's meanings. But for Kelly it is a construct which may have different meanings for different people even though there is an agreed verbal label.

Another argument against the classic distinction between emotions and cognitions is that *the* emotions do not exist as entities. They are no more 'facts' than anything else. Rom Harré (1982) spells this out. He suggests that what really enables us to agree on the meanings of emotions is their link with our cultural mores. He cites several emotions which few of us would claim to experience. For instance, *accidie* was a common emotion in the Middle Ages and was closely bound up with religious duty. You experienced accidie when you failed in your duty. This did not lead to guilt or shame as it might today, but to 'a kind of gloom' or, as the Oxford Dictionary says, 'sloth, torpor'. There was also *angor*, meaning anguish in 1711 or 'a feeling of anxiety and constriction in the precordial region'. Can we recognize this today? If we did, we would not call it that.

Are we to conclude that these emotions have just disappeared? That seems unlikely. Could it be that the same bodily states are construed and given different names? Perhaps it is more complicated than that. Rom Harré suggests we have to look at what society suggests to us is important. The vapours disappeared at the end of the Victorian era, perhaps because of the new role women were finding for themselves. Psychiatrists report that hysterical conversion symptoms so common at the time of Freud are now very rare indeed. Perhaps this is because Freud's ideas about the power of 'the unconscious' gained widespread popularity and so people became more psychologically literate. In the same way, accidie and angor disappeared as the social scene changed.

Likewise there are words to describe emotional states in other languages which appear to have no literal translation into English. Does this mean the English never experience these emotions? For instance, there are the German states of *gemütlichkeit* or *angst*. What complicated emotional states these are. *Gemütlichkeit* is the German word for '(the quality of the) good-natured, sanguine, easy-going disposition; good nature; kindliness; geniality; pleasantness; cordiality; sentiment, tenderness of feeling; freedom from pecuniary cares; comfortableness'. *Angst* throws together 'anguish; anxiety, fear'.

If we impose our own personal meaning of emotion on to someone else, we may be guilty of misunderstanding them. Just as the imposing of traits on to others stifles individuality, so may the imposing of emotional labels. Helen Jones (1985) argues that we should be careful when using the term 'depression' to describe someone's state. Every person who says they are depressed will, when listened to, provide their own idiosyncratic picture of the experience. This does not mean that there is no common denominator amongst all the 'depressions', but that the realities personally experienced may differ. In personal construct psychology, depression relates to professional constructs such as *constriction* – the personal world has been made smaller and smaller – and in content terms experiencing of the self is at the 'bad' poles of many of our constructs.

In just the same way we may all have some common meaning we attribute to the construct 'idiosyncratic' but for some of us this may be a good thing to be whilst for others it is highly undesirable. The issue here is that *the verbal label should never be equated with the underlying meaning of the construct.* Construing is about experiencing our private worlds.

One reason why people cling to the idea that Kelly did not deal adequately with 'the emotions' is that it was some years after the publication of his two volumes that he decided to spell out his views more clearly. Another may be that this dualism is deeply embedded in Western cultural mores. 'Feelings' are to do with the physiology of the body whereas 'thinking' takes place in the brain. Freud and psychoanalysis focus mainly on the feeling aspects of the person and deal less well with thinking. But no one keeps shouting that this is wrong and that Freud only produced 'an emotional theory'. So why should Kelly be so misrepresented? He may not have dealt as explicitly and in such detail with emotion as he did with cognition. But to say he did not deal with emotion is a calumny.

Don Bannister sought to counter this argument once and for all in 1977 in his paper 'The logic of passion'. He argued that Kelly had every right to do what he liked within his own theory. He chose to view the person as a complete entity and as a form of motion. That meant there was no place for the study of 'bits' of the person so beloved of psychology textbooks. But the kernel of the discussion was that Kelly's philosophy makes every idea an invitation.

> Most psychological theories have not sought to challenge the picture of people as segmented into thought and feeling. Indeed they have not even seen it as *a picture*, they have taken it as 'real' and worked within the boundaries thereby set. Kelly was truly adventurous in abandoning the construct and offering alternative ways of interpreting experience. The alternative he offered, the construct of 'change', is open to criticism, it is an invitation which we are free to refuse. The least sensible or gracious response to his invitation is not to see that it was being made and to categorise Kelly as a man who did not understand 'emotion' and who thereby constructed a merely 'cognitive' theory. (Bannister, 1977: 36)

Is It a Cognitive Theory?

So we come to the related argument that personal construct theory is a cognitive theory. People say it is about how we 'think' our world into being rather than how we experience our world as a being in motion. Kelly did actually start out theorizing in cognitive terms. In 1938 he was using what he called 'rational' therapy, which he said aimed to show the client how to 'think through' his difficulty. But, even then, as later, he saw therapy and diagnosis as being combined and the whole process as being an educative one.

Nowadays, those who find personal construct theory a useful framework within which to carry out our work continue to resist the attempt to place it within the category of cognitive theory. Some, including myself, feel very strongly that to take just one aspect of the person (their thought processes) and leave all other aspects of experiencing out of the picture leaves an impoverished, emasculated theory. Joseph Rychlak, a Kelly ex-student, is of the opinion that there is no better example of a dialectical theory than Kelly's personal construct theory. However, he 'fears that there is a tendency today on the part of some interpreters of Kelly to distort the true spirit of his theory by turning it into a mediational conception along the lines of what is today called "cognitive psychology". This psychology is in reality a continuation of the mechanistic, efficient-cause theories of the past, theories which George Kelly rejected and actively opposed' (Rychlak, 1978: 261).

However, there are others (and these include some who say they espouse the personal construct model) who hail George Kelly as the creator of the cognitive theoretical model. The first such statement came from Walter Mischel, one of George Kelly's students, in a personal tribute to Kelly:

> That George Kelly was a very deep, original, refreshing voice was always evident to all who knew him well. What has surprised me was not the brilliance with which he first spoke but the accuracy with which he anticipated the directions into which psychology would move two decades later. (Mischel, 1980: 85)

It is interesting to compare this statement on the prophetic nature of Kelly's psychology with that of Warren (1989, see Chapter 2) concerning the prophetic nature of Kelly's philosophy. Mischel continues, 'Long before "cognitive psychology" existed, Kelly created a truly cognitive theory of personality, a theory in which how people construe is at the core' (Mischel, 1980: 86).

Jahoda (1988) argues that those involved with personal construct theory misunderstand the changes that have taken place in the use of the word 'cognitive' and are making a song and dance about nothing.

> What then is Kelly's approach? Above all Kelly is a cognitivist, in the modern sense of this term. In the dim past when I first studied psychology, the term 'cognitive' was, following Aristotle, understood as one of the three basic faculties of the soul, the other two being conative

> and emotive. *At present, the use of the term is confused and confusing.* While some cognitivists still adhere to the old distinction, the broader view that Kelly had in mind is gradually gaining ground. . . . This modern concept is best understood in contrast to behaviourism, that relegates all internal events and processes to the 'black box', by definition outside its concerns. Modern cognitivism, however, makes the entire content of the black box its exclusive concern in the recognition that all psychological phenomena rest on symbolic representations in the mind, including not only perceiving, learning, thinking and remembering but also desire and feeling *because they too are tied to cognitions.* (Jahoda, 1988: 3; italics mine)

Jahoda may well be correct that modern cognitivism is moving towards Kelly's corner. But Kelly's definition of anxiety, for example, is not 'tied to cognitions'. In fact, we are said to feel anxiety because we are *unable* to construe the event with which we are confronted. Jahoda may have a broad definition of cognition, but the arguments still abound that castigate Kelly for not dealing with emotion. We now seem to be in the strange situation that cognitive theory deals with emotion and personal construct theory does not.

In 1990, there appeared in the *International Journal of Personal Construct Psychology* two articles on this issue. First, there was W. G. Warren's paper 'Is personal construct psychology a cognitive psychology?' This was followed by Adams-Webber's reply 'Personal construct theory and cognitive science'. Then, in 1991, Warren exercised the right of reply in 'Rising up from down under: a response to Adams-Webber on cognitive psychology and personal construct theory'.

In his first paper, Warren concludes that a) it is very difficult to say what is and what is not a cognitive process; b) personal construct theory focuses on the individual making sense of the world by imposing meaning on it rather than the ways in which we interpret events; c) the philosophy underlying personal construct theory can be traced back to the Greeks and that of cognitive psychology cannot. Adams-Webber (1990) gives a heated defence of cognitive psychology and draws from Warren (1991) the feeling that he is being accused of setting up 'a straw man'.

What comes over clearly is the feeling that these two men are talking different languages. The argument does little to resolve the issue. Perhaps we should take Adams-Webber's concluding remark as the final word: 'It appears highly unlikely that anyone who is thoroughly familiar with personal construct theory could entertain the preemptive position that it is "nothing but" a form of cognitive psychology' (Adams-Webber, 1990: 419).

The Role of Society

It is an often-cited criticism of personal construct theory that it does not take sufficient account of the social context within which people construe and need to reconstrue, and the effects the social context has on the development of their constructions.

To set the scene, Kelly was of the opinion that 'the take-off point of a social psychology' was the Sociality Corollary.

> By attempting to place at the forefront of psychology the understanding of personal constructs, and by recognizing, as a corollary of our Fundamental Postulate, the subsuming of other people's construing efforts as the basis for social interaction, we have said that social psychology must be a psychology of interpersonal understandings, not merely a psychology of common understandings. (Kelly 1991, Vol. 1: 67)

The criticisms of personal construct theory in relation to social contexts are at two levels. One is to do with Kelly's apparent lack of awareness or acknowledgement of the *importance* of the social context in which individuals develop. The other is that the theory is itself unable to describe social structures and show how they influence personal construing.

The Importance of Social Contexts

Taking the first type of criticism, the lack of awareness or acknowledgement of social factors, we have Procter and Parry, who say:

> In each type of society the dominant ideology reflects the needs and concerns of the power-holding group. In this context, *any* action or statement is seen as having ideological implications. Thus, psychological theories which claim to be politically neutral are making an unwitting statement in support of the *status quo*.
>
> Kelly himself seems almost entirely unaware of these issues. Where he does mention social class it is with a touching naïveté about its importance in influencing an individual's view of the world. (Procter and Parry, 1978: 157)

With what we now know about George Kelly's social class background, we may charge him with many crimes, but naïveté about the importance of social class as an influence on the individual is not one of them.

But there have been many other criticisms in the same vein. Such comments would seem to ignore the hundred pages or so in Volume 2 (1991) in which Kelly explicitly talks about the importance of the social context within which a person develops. From his point of view:

> The client is not merely the product of his culture, but it has undoubtedly provided him with much evidence of what is 'true' and much of the data which his personal construct system has had to keep in systematic order. (Kelly, 1991, Vol. 2: 92)

But in 1963, perhaps conscious of what people had been saying, he wrote this in 'The autobiography of a theory':

> But to believe that man is the author of his destiny is not to deny that he may be tragically limited by his circumstances. I saw too many unfortunate youngsters, some of them literally starving in that depression-ridden dust bowl, for me not to be aware of their tragic limitations. Clearly there were many things they might have liked to do that circumstances would not permit. But, nevertheless, this is not to say that they were victims of circumstances. However much there was denied them there was still an infinity of possibilities open to them. The task was to generate the imagination needed to envision those possibilities. And this is a point of departure for a psychology of man, the canons of nineteenth century scientific determinism notwithstanding. (Kelly, 1969a: 50)

He would not be shaken from his fundamental theoretical postulate which states that it is 'a *person's*' processes in which he is interested and not '*society's*' processes. However, his awareness of the importance of the social context is everywhere. Following on from the above quote, he proceeds to enumerate seven ways in which the therapist may identify the client's socio-economic class. After this he says:

> Instead of spending too much time on identification of socio-economic class membership, however, the clinical psychologist is usually better advised to turn his attention to the ethnic groupings with which the client is identified. (Kelly, 1991, Vol. 2: 97)

There are then five descriptions of how the therapist might carry out this identification. These include obvious ones such as racial and national extraction and church membership. Other less obvious ones are typically American, such as 'migration routes'. These are again followed by fifteen ways in which he suggests that 'frequently the clinician finds it most profitable of all to make some direct assessment of the cultural–experiential determinants of personal constructs'.

His life-long concern for social context can be seen from the paper he wrote when he was twenty-five in 1930 entitled 'The social inheritance' (Kelly, 1930). This led Marie Jahoda to remark 'There is, after all, a Sociality Corollary, and nobody who has read Kelly's essay on social inheritance . . . and is familiar with his general approach, could doubt his deep personal concern with social reality' (Jahoda, 1988: 9).

It is clear that Kelly thought it very important for the clinician to find out as much as possible about the cultural context in which the client had developed. *But*, this was to identify not simply the 'pressures' that had been brought to bear on them, but what they had made of the social constraints they encountered.

His actual view about the nature of society is given an interesting twist in an interview with me. Talking about society in a general sense, he says:

> I suppose everyone wants to do something about society. I suppose it represents a sort of paranoid tendency to blame his own fate on the facts of society and I suppose I am not exempt from that sort of paranoia. (Kelly, 1966)

In a talk Don Bannister gave in 1981, he says that he discussed where Kelly would like personal construct theory to go. Kelly surprised him by opting for politics. Unfortunately, Kelly died soon after that meeting.

But in the quote above concerning doing something about society, Kelly was talking as a person and not as an exponent of his theory. Procter and Parry are correct in saying that personal construct theory is politically neutral but incorrect in deducing that this makes it 'an unwitting statement in support of the *status quo*'. As Don Bannister pointed out, Kelly's philosophy is of constructive alternativism. This denies the possibility of an absolute truth. This means that there are not indisputable religious, social or political truths either. He says that this is

> a basic political value embedded in personal construct theory . . . Constructive alternativism argues for an open society in which the pursuit of alternatives is central to the way in which we live. Political doctrines favouring authoritarian forms of social structure require the acceptance of indisputable truths, indisputable 'realities'. (Bannister, 1981: 6)

The Description of Social Structure

The second basis of the social complaint levelled against Kelly is that he did not also produce a theory of sociology. Jahoda (1988) quotes Henri Tajfel et al. (1984) as saying that a social psychology 'can and must include in its theoretical and research preoccupations a direct concern with the relationship between human psychological functionings and *the large-scale social processes and events which shape this functioning and are shaped by it*' (italics mine). Jahoda then goes on to talk about Moscovici's (1983) emphasis on Durkheim's *représentations sociales*.

A short while before the conference at which Jahoda gave her paper, I had carried out an analysis of the relationship between Kelly's constructs and Durkheim's representations (Fransella, 1984). It was clear that there are similarities between Durkheim's individual representations and personal constructs, although the latter are far more complex. But Durkheim's 'collective representations' were seen by him as something quite different. He spelt out the difference between the individual and collective representation as follows:

> Society is a reality *sui generis*; it has its own peculiar characteristics, which are not found elsewhere and which are not met again in the same form in all the rest of the universe. The representations which express it have a wholly different content from purely individual ones and we may rest assured in advance that *the first adds something to the second.* (Durkheim, 1961: 16; italics mine)

Or again, even more clearly:

> The psychologist who restricts himself to the ego cannot emerge to find the non ego. Collective life is not born from individual life, but it is, on the contrary, *the second which is born from the first.* (Durkheim, 1933: 279; italics mine)

To draw a distinction between individual and collective construing and place the emphasis on the latter is eminently understandable considering that Durkheim is described as one of the founding fathers of sociology.

On the basis of the foregoing, the conclusion must surely be that Kelly is being criticized for providing a 'personal' and not a 'social' construct theory. But Kelly made it quite explicit at the outset that he was concerned with the psychology of the 'person'. As Jahoda says, there has yet to be a theory that can properly incorporate the perspectives of individual psychology and social structures. Kelly would agree with that, and says: 'Some of the phenomena which physiological systems seek to explain or which sociological systems seek to explain are admittedly outside our present field of interest and we feel no obligation to account for them within this particular theoretical structure' (Kelly, 1991, Vol. 1: 33).

It needs also to be borne in mind that Kelly was not a sociological innocent. He had studied sociology in 1926 and completed a master's thesis on industrial workers' use of leisure time. He therefore knew something of what he was talking about. He spells out the distinction between psychology and sociology as early as 1932 in 'Understandable Psychology'. In the chapter on 'Social Psychology' he first of all emphasizes his view that 'man lives in groups' and the importance of social interaction by saying:

> *'you can have no such thing as an individual unless you have a group'*. That is equivalent to saying that there is no egg without a chicken.
>
> It is only because of his social contacts that man acquires status as an individual. It is through a social or inter-individual relationship that he is able to come into existence in the first place. . . . There are no individuals until there are other individuals for them to be related to and distinguished from. The group and individual are two aspects of the same thing. (Kelly, 1932: 184)

He then proceeds to talk about the 'group mind'. He rejects the sociologist's view that there is a group mind distinct from the minds of the individuals comprising the group. He asks 'What is mind?' The answer is that it is the underlying pattern of cognitive processes. This leads to the next question, 'Can there be an underlying pattern of cognitive processes of a group?' And, if so, what is it like? He then goes on to answer his last question:

> The cognitive processes of the group are no other than the organic processes of the individual members. But is there an underlying pattern for these processes which is not to be seen in any one member? Yes! . . . A lone voter cannot deadlock an election. A bride does not go on a honeymoon alone. The process of group behavior is nothing but the behavior of individual members, although the pattern may be super-individual. In this sense, then, we can say there is a group mind. But wait, we should be careful not to jump to conclusions. *The group mind is not a separate organism, not a separate process, not a separate will, not a separate force from that of the individual. It is a super-pattern into which the individual sub-patterns fit. . . . The group mind is a situation into which individual tendencies are so combined as to make their effect violently felt by all.* (Kelly, 1932: 185–6)

Having talked about the nature of language, of sociology, and of personality, he ends with a definition of social psychology:

> The science of social psychology lies between that of sociology, anthropology, and ethnology on the one hand and that of psychology on the other. It is a study, not merely of the individual mind, but of the influences which play upon the individual mind, particularly other human minds to which adjustment must be made. Its terms are less well defined than those of psychology, and it cannot lay claim to being such an exact science. Its field, however, is infinitely broad – and infinitely interesting. (Kelly, 1932: 195)

All the foregoing evidence suggests that Kelly placed great importance on social contexts, that he was not naïve, and that he gave considerable coverage to them all.

Reflexivity

Closely linked to this discussion of the extent to which Kelly takes sufficient account of the social context within which a person construes and reconstrues, is the issue of the extent to which personal construct theory is really as reflexive as it thinks itself to be.

Holland (1981) argues that reflexivity should be used for a theory being applied to itself as much as to a theorist or therapist applying a theory to themselves. He calls the latter 'weak' reflexivity and finds it unsatisfactory on a number of counts. 'Weak reflexivity operates as a negative criterion in the sense that it rules out forms of knowledge that do not operate at a human level.' He is right in this. Holland argues for the application of a 'strong' reflexivity. This would involve having a more superordinate form of knowledge applied to the theory so that it could come to 'know itself'. Only in this way can one have a basis for radical criticism. Only by using sociopsychological analysis can the theory move on. Only by seeing the theory in a social context, in the context of other theories such as psychoanalytic and behaviourist ones, can personal construct theory 'know itself'.

Few would disagree with that either. It is an important point. In some sense it is what we are doing when thinking about the ways in which personal construct theory is still a radical theory forty years after its launch. We are construing the theory as one theory among others and so looking at its current standing.

I am less in harmony with one of Holland's other points, though. He seems to be suggesting, as others have done before and since, that Kelly was arguing that if everyone became a personal construct theorist all would be light and joy. Holland says Kelly's (or his followers') weak reflexivity 'is a metaphor of liberal pluralism with the prospect of increasing consensus and harmony'.

I have made this point before and unashamedly do so again. Kelly did not say that a personal construct theorist *should* live the life of someone who constantly looks inwards into himself or outwards into the construing of another. He simply said that if you want to understand yourself or someone else this is a useful way of going about it. Psychotherapists certainly aim to do this when working as professionals. But at a non-professional level, no one can live an abstract theory every hour of the day. For that is what personal construct theory is. It has no substance; no content. We, as individuals, create the content of our lives. Kelly made one of his serious jokes on this theme. He said his nightmare was of waking up one morning and finding that his best friend was a psychotherapist. As individuals we do not go through each day trying to understand the ways in which each person we encounter looks at things that may be different from the way we see things. If you do this too often with friends, they soon say things like 'Now you are psychologizing me! Stop it!' It is only when we are in a professional capacity that we do this.We may take on the philosophy as a personal way of looking at the world if we find it useful. But few of us live our lives at a philosophical level. I may believe in my heart of hearts that there are always alternative ways of looking at an event, but when that event is that someone has just slotted themselves into a parking space which I was lined up for, to hell with alternatives, I'm just plain mad!

Inadequate Attention to the Development of the Child

Another constant criticism is that Kelly did not spell out how a person develops their personal construing system. He certainly did not do so. In my opinion, he never set out to do so. Whereas he was at pains to say how essential contact with others was for our development of self, he was at no pains to say why he offered no theory of child development. The words 'development' and 'children' do not appear in the index of the two volumes. There are a few entries under 'child', but these refer to factual details.

George Kelly saw the entire life-span as an anticipatory, developmental, evolutionary, process. One of the most common questions from those coming to know personal construct theory is 'Where does construing start?' Over the years, it has become more and more apparent that it does not start anywhere. One can discount some point in a baby's life since it is known that the foetus can discriminate between events. Then, what about the ovum and the sperm? But why start there? The more one continues this exercise the further one goes. Plants can be seen as construing. Their roots and stems move in the direction of light or nutriment. And so on. Those interested in artificial intelligence once tried to carry out this exercise by looking at Kelly's theory in detail. The theory is in excellent shape. The only problem came when there had to be something that anticipated something in the first place. These researchers were forced back to the notion that a fundamental difference between living and non-living matter is that living matter construes.

In 'The psychology of optimal man', Kelly actually speculates about where a biological postulate would take one. It would go something like this:

> It is the nature of life to be channelized by the ways events are anticipated. While I am not prepared to defend this assumption with great skill or the weight of much evidence, it does intrigue me and I cannot help but wonder where we would be if we ventured to start from such a premise. Particularly, I wonder what a psychotherapist would be led to

> do or what goals he would envision for the outcomes of his efforts. (Kelly, 1980: 29)

Kelly goes on to speculate about such frequently asked questions as 'Does personal construct theory have any practical application to rats?' He goes on to say:

> It is sufficient for a paper dealing with the goals of psychotherapy merely to suggest the notion that possibly, quite apart from psychology, life itself is essentially an anticipation of events to come. This is a more venturesome postulate than the one from which the psychology of personal constructs was launched. But from it may spring some additional ideas about the whole of psychology, as well as about the goals of psychotherapy. (Kelly, 1980: 29)

So development does not *start*, it is there from the beginning. In a sense it has no special meaning, it is just part of the living process. For the person, Kelly deals with it in the Experience Corollary, and says:

> As one's anticipations or hypotheses are successively revised in the light of the unfolding sequence of events, the construct system undergoes a progressive evolution. The person reconstrues. This is experience. (Kelly, 1991, Vol. 1: 51)

The absence of a theory of development was no doubt deliberate on Kelly's part. His theory has no room for compartments or categories into which we can slot people. He would have none of 'stages of development' or 'fixations' during childhood. A child is as much a construing being as an adult. There are obviously substantial differences, but these are covered by the theoretical constructs themselves – such as preverbal construing, dependency and the like. In support of the suggestion that Kelly deliberately did not talk of the developing child as being different from the developing adult is the fact that he spent a great deal of his early years as a clinical psychologist working with children. A browse through his writings shows just how many of his examples are to do with children, not to mention his years at Fort Hays. This suggests he would certainly have adequate personal knowledge to write a theory of child development, had he so wished.

Development is thus a process that continues throughout life. Development, in personal construct terms, does not necessarily mean 'for the better'. We can become less able to control our world by being more wrong than right in our prediction of events. Sometimes we make such a mess of things that we need the help of a psychotherapist to get on the move again. But there are definitely no personal construct 'stages' through which a child *should* pass on its way to adulthood. The point has often been made that 'stages' of development are in any case in the eye of the psychologist and not in the eye of the individual doing the developing.

Vaughan and Pfenninger point out that in denying the usefulness of stages of development, Kelly was not saying that people have nothing in common as they go through life. Of course they do and it is often useful to investigate those commonalities. These authors say:

> This does not at all negate commonalities among persons in their development; it simply invites researchers to integrate individualism and contextualism, an integration that we believe represents one of Kelly's most monumental achievements. (Vaughan and Pfenninger, 1994: 187)

Some work with children has been carried out since 1955, and has started to show how construing changes as a child develops. It is easy to see how such work could lead to Piagetian-type stages of conceptual development.

Before leaving this subject, I want to give an example from Kelly of one of the few occasions in which he actually gives an account of how he thinks a child might be studied. He cites a teacher's notes after a particular episode at school. Four-year-old Larry is not joining in the group activities such as singing or story-telling.

> She comments, 'He is wild, imaginative, and appears totally absorbed in a private game.' She goes on to say,
>
> 'In a father role the following day, Larry again had difficulty making contact with his peers. He insisted upon throwing every single tiny piece of equipment into the toy sink. Sally, who was playing a mother role, was furious and kept putting things away. Finally, after Larry had thrown everything into the sink for the third time, Sally left the game. Larry then climbed up a tall divider, transgressing a teacher-imposed boundary. There, at my suggestion, he "repaired the roof" and then climbed down. I had hoped to give him a reason for being up there and a way of getting down without losing face. He seemed quite willing to go along with my suggestion, but the game he and Sally had been playing had ended abruptly and apparently inconclusively.'
>
> Two months later Mrs. Upton comments:
>
> 'Larry and I had a conversation about hunting during which I mentioned that pygmies used darts dipped in poison for hunting and for defence. This intrigued Larry. Half an hour later he approached me with a stick and jabbed it into my leg.
>
> "There, Don, she's dead."
>
> I slumped over, playing my part in the game.
>
> Larry became very excited and shouted, "Let's bury her, Don!" As he tried to pick me up I collapsed on the floor and Larry started shovelling imaginary sand on top of me. Sally came into the room and, finding me "dead" threw her arms around my neck and started to cry. I reassured her, and then noticed Larry curled up on the floor behind me.

> "I wonder what you are doing?"
> "I'm just lying here feeling sorry for you, Mrs. Upton."' (Kelly, 1970b: 263–4)

Kelly comments on this last episode seeing it as a completed experiment designed by the child and as having significance for him.

> How much more psychologically significant this was than to have offered a guilty apology for what he had done. (Kelly, 1970b: 265)

It seems quite likely that this is how Kelly wanted us to understand the world of children and not to use artificial stages that start as being descriptive and all too soon become prescriptive.

Personal Construct Theory and Constructivism

Constructivism seems to be everywhere. The Americans have even changed the name of the *International Journal of Personal Construct Psychology* to the *Journal of Constructivist Psychology.* It would not be correct to call Kelly 'the first constructivist' because its roots have been traced back through the centuries.

Interestingly, some have said its origins go back to Brentano's act psychology, and Kelly talks in 1932 about Brentano indicating that constructivism and constructive alternativism have the same or similar roots. Kelly talks as follows:

> Franz Brentano (1838–1917) of Italian descent was born and lived in Germany. He is important because we may directly trace to him one of the important systems of psychology of the last century. Following in the train which we have hinted at from the philosophy of Leibnitz he maintained that mental phenomena are to be thought of as acts; hence the name given this system of psychology – act psychology. We do not see the color green, but we *act* in such a way as to imply such a phenomenon. The sensation of sound is not sound itself, but it is an *act* in which sound is imminent. Notice the distinction between the sensation and the thing which is sensed. The former is an *act*; the latter is a *content.* Of course the content is the intention of the act. The act stands for the content. (Kelly, 1932: 220)

Apart from this history, the European antecedents of constructivism are people like Frederick Bartlett with his famous book on *Remembering* (1932) and, of course, Jean Piaget, whose book *The Construction of Reality in the Child* was first published in English in 1954.

There is little to distinguish constructivism as generally discussed from Kelly's constructive alternativism, although the latter offers more. They are similar in that both see the person as having no direct contact with reality; we only know reality by the ways in which we impose our own meaning on it. This stems directly from Immanual Kant. What seems likely is that the word 'constructivism' comes directly from Kelly's philosophy of *constructive* alternativism.

From the point of view of psychotherapy I see problems developing, for those who espouse constructivism see it as a substitute for a psychological theory – they appear to be substituting a philosophy for a psychological theory.

I see no problem at all in personal construct theory being subsumed under the label *constructivist.* It could be the 'strong reflexivity' that Holland (1981) is seeking. It seems to be little more than constructive alternativism re-writ. Vasco (1994), for instance, studied the views of people who called themselves 'constructivists'. He found some agreement in that they thought there should be no pre-determined goals for the client, that there should be no 'correct view' of the problem and that the client should be encouraged to explore himself or herself actively.

The issue is about what is happening in the name of constructivism. It seems as if some people are heralding the re-birth of eclecticism and saying that as long as you are a constructivist and abide by that philosophy, you can do what you like, certainly in the realm of psychotherapy.

Under this rubric of constructivism, many are 'inventing' their own individual psychotherapeutic practice and, in so doing, are moving into areas that are the antithesis of personal construct theory. For example, Michael Mahoney says, 'From the constructivist perspective, the process of psychotherapy is not essentially different from the process of any other form of human inquiry and learning' (Mahoney, 1988: 307). Personal construct psychology would not argue with that. Mahoney then outlines his own scheme for individual psychotherapy. Under 'assessment' he has 'Basic psychometrics of choice . . .': a return to the psychometrics that Kelly fought to eliminate because he saw them as dehumanizing. This serves simply as an example of the atheoretical stance that some constructivists seem to be taking as regards psychotherapy. Mahoney, for instance, later (1991) changed his views on assessment and is now developing his own psychological theory.

In my view, there is nothing wrong with Mahoney or anyone else doing anything they like providing it is in line with some ethical code. That is not the issue. But constructivism is a philosophical system that cannot guide psychotherapy. A philosophical system guides a psychological theory. It would be rather like having a 'behaviourism' therapy. That would be fine as a set of criteria that place it apart from psychodynamic theory, but it offers in itself no theory with which to understand the client's problems or help the client towards a way of solving those problems.

If personal construct theory is allowed to be subsumed under the umbrella of constructivism as if it were *nothing but* constructivist, Kelly's philosophy may well survive, but his theory will sink without trace.

Those who would like to read more on this complex issue are referred to *Constructivism in Psychotherapy* (Neimeyer and Mahoney, 1995).

Summary

Criticisms come both from outside personal construct psychotherapy and from within. From outside there are those who fight for it to be construed as a 'cognitive therapy'. That is a theme that has recurred throughout this book. In the final analysis, the argument seems to be becoming one about the actual meaning of the construct 'cognitive'. 'Personal construct theory is not a cognitive theory, but a theory about how the human process flows, how it strives in new directions as well as in old, and how it may dare for the first time to reach into the depths of newly perceived dimensions of human life' (Kelly, 1973; in manuscript version, p. 5).

Another long-standing debate has been about the extent to which Kelly focused on the individual at the expense of the individual within a social context. If the discussion is about the social context only, then I think it can fairly be argued that Kelly spent considerable energy demonstrating how an individual has to be understood within their own social environment. However, if the discussion is at a more abstract level, to do with society, then there is no argument. The critics are correct, Kelly was quite explicit in saying that he was not writing a sociology, only a psychology.

With his vast practical experience of working with children, it is strange, at first sight, that he did not apply his theory to child development. One could say 'But didn't he do enough for one man in one life-time?' But there is more to it than that. He did not describe a theory of child development because he was against any such categorization. Children are creating their own selves just as adults are; they are conducting their own experiments and so forth. There is no direct evidence that he deliberately ignored the 'stages of development' approach, but it seems very likely.

There is pressure, from both those who practise personal construct psychotherapy and those who are critics of that approach, to subsume it explicitly under the philosophy of constructivism. Constructivism is a philosophy which has yet to be shown to be fundamentally different from Kelly's own philosophy of constructive alternativism. The issue is becoming one in which 'constructivists' believe that that is all one needs to be – seeing the client as having the answers, as having created their own world and so forth. Many personal construct psychotherapists would argue that if you are going to carry out such an important task as trying to help another human being solve their personal difficulties, then you need more than the guidance of a philosophy. You need a good, sound, complex theory.

5

The Overall Influence of George Kelly

There are three broad areas of Kelly's influence on counselling and psychotherapy to be covered in this chapter. These are his influence on: (1) current psychotherapies; (2) the methods of therapy and of assessment that have been developed since his death; and (3) the application of his theory and methods to therapy and counselling for those with specific problems.

The first section is largely a summary of what has already been covered in previous chapters. The second and third sections contain mainly new material. A large amount of work has been carried out over the last three decades, so there has been a very great deal to choose from. Selection has been made on the basis of methods and theories that may be of use for the *practice* of psychotherapy.

Kelly's Personal Influence

I think it would be fair to say that George Kelly's personal influence was not always positive. He made no attempt whatever to persuade anyone to use his theoretical approach, and some say he actively discouraged it. For instance, Rue Cromwell says:

> Kelly never failed to emphasize that he wanted commitment and courage to explore, innovate, try on the new idea or role . . . to see how it fits. Repeatedly, as I sat in as the assistant in his clinical practicum supervisory sessions, he would emphasize to the beginning practicum students that he did not approve of following a recipe – including 'Kelly's recipe'. (Cromwell, personal communication)

Also, his treatment of some of his students put them off his approach. Esther Cava says:

> One thing that is too bad in a way is that because of how they perceived Kelly as a person so many of his students, once they left school, did not want to have anything to do with his theory because it was *his* theory. (Cava, personal communication)

Against this there are very many who have gone on to become leaders, not only in the world of personal construct psychology but also in the larger world of psychology itself.

Kelly's Theory and Philosophy in the Larger World of Science

Constructive Alternativism and the Constructivist Movement

Kelly was not only a prime influence in establishing the constructivist emphasis in psychology in general and psychotherapy in particular, dating back to the 1930s and 1940s. He also gave the person integrity. Our views of the world are our own, and he gave us personal control and responsibility over our actions. The client, and indeed all of us, conduct our own experiments by 'behaving'. Our behaviour mirrors our current understanding of our world. Sometimes we make appalling mistakes in our experiments. But experimenters we are, nonetheless. I therefore think a further point of Kellyian constructivism should be added to those mentioned in the last chapter. That is, 'the therapist seeks to understand what it is that the client is putting to the test by behaving in the way that he or she does'.

Organic Constructions versus the Biological Postulate

Kelly said explicitly that he was concerned with the psychology of the person and the psychology only. This was so crucial to him that he put it into his fundamental postulate, which says: 'A person's processes are *psychologically* channelized by the ways in which they anticipate events.' Leave our genes to the geneticist, our biochemistry to the biochemist, our nervous system to the neurologist and so on.

Kelly saw that espousing some organic causation of problems too often means looking to drugs or brain surgery for cures *at the expense of* helping the person take charge of their own life. Lest someone should want to push this too far, I must add that this does not mean a personal construct psychotherapist would never want their client to have drugs. These can be very helpful with, for instance, the client who is so depressed that they have given up communicating altogether. But drugs here are a means to an end – to help the client start to share their construing with someone – and not an end in themselves.

Kelly's emphasis on a purely psychological constructivism means that we, as psychotherapists, are free to look at problems that some see as 'basically organic', such as dysphasia, stuttering, schizophrenia or depression from the viewpoint of the person experiencing these things. It needs to be remembered that Kelly includes all emotional experiencing under the term 'psychological'.

No one would deny that dysphasia, for instance, is most often caused by some damage to the cerebral cortex. In the past help has come from speech therapists focusing on their speech. But Brumfitt and Clarke (1983) give as much attention to the feelings and overall construing of their clients. They see these clients as having suffered a major loss and as having a grief reaction. Brumfitt (1985) also discusses how she uses grids with such clients who have very restricted speech. (The development of theoretical and practical personal construct approaches to the specific problems of stuttering, schizophrenia and depression are covered later in this chapter.)

An area that can only be touched on here, because there is no 'approach' and no 'evidence', concerns the theory's application to the treatment of cancer. An example of Kelly's breadth of vision was to see the whole body as a construing process. In his 1955 work (1955a), he gives the example of the 'construing' of the digestive system. As mentioned in the last chapter, Kelly even speculates about where the creation of a biological postulate might take one. He said it might go something like: 'It is the nature of life to be channelized by the ways events are anticipated.'

So, using Kelly's breadth of vision, we can look at the cells that make up our bodies as construing processes. Perhaps they go along happily reproducing themselves in harmony with others as they have always done because it is in this way that life is most meaningful for them. But on occasion they work on the opposite pole of the construct to do with reproducing themselves 'in their own patch' only. This, in turn, becomes the most meaningful thing to do for some reason.

At one level that can all be seen as a load of nonsense. But just suppose it has a grain of 'truth' in it somewhere? It is an hypothesis from a theory and all theories lead to suggestions about the process of change. We would need to help the cells reconstrue so that they could behave as they used to. Meditation or visualization or other forms of 'looking into' bodily processes could be and are used. The malfunctioning cells are 'entered into' by the client at some deep level.

No one claims that these approaches 'cure' cancer. All that people are saying is that it does seem to have been of some help to some patients. Who knows where this might lead? To the madhouse some will say. Others perhaps may want to explore this avenue further. For a discussion of this whole area see, for example,

Simonton and Creighton's book *Getting Well Again* (1978). These authors look at some of the evidence that has accrued over the years.

Kelly's Influence on Approaches to Psychotherapy

The Development of Cognitive Therapy

Many cite Kelly as the originator of cognitive therapy. For instance, the eminent psychologist Walter Mischel has already been mentioned as seeing Kelly as the first cognitive psychologist. He comments further on Kelly's influence thus:

> Virtually every point of George Kelly's theorizing for the 1950s ... proved to be a prophetic preface for the psychology of the 1970s and – it seems safe to predict now – for many years to come. ... There is reason to hope that the current moves toward a hyphenated cognitive-behavioral approach will help fill in the grand outlines that Kelly sketched years before anyone else even realized the need. (Mischel, 1980: 86)

The argument against personal construct theory being called a cognitive theory has already been given in the previous chapter. What we have here, though, is the fact that, whether or not personal construct theory can be placed in that category, cognitive therapy was created and has flourished. George Kelly would not mind that at all. He might even take some caustic pleasure in having his name attached to it. But, accept it as describing what he and his theory were about – he would not.

His eyes would certainly have twinkled at the idea recently expressed that cognitive theory might be seen as just an extension of personal construct theory! As Lister-Ford and Pokorny have written:

> It is a moot point whether personal construct therapy belongs to the cognitive therapies, as one of the variations that have arisen from the work of Kelly. Is it really any more than another version of the use of his work to provide a different framework for changing behaviour? (Lister-Ford and Pokorny, 1994: 151)

The conclusion is that Kelly profoundly influenced the field of psychotherapy by spawning a group of therapies that have all become influential in their own right. Lister-Ford and Pokorny say that 'In 1955 Kelly put the emphasis on how people give meaning to their world, and the foundation stone of cognitive therapy was laid. Now there are about seventeen cognitive therapies' (1994: 147). Probably the best known are rational emotive therapy (Ellis, 1958), cognitive therapy in relation to depression (Beck et al.,

1979) and Meichenbaum (1977) with his cognitive-behavioural therapy. David Winter (1992) gives a detailed account of these and their relationship to personal construct therapy.

Influence on Existential Therapies

One important figure in the development of the existential therapies is James Bugental – yet another of Kelly's students. In his book *The Search for Existential Identity*, he says:

> George A Kelly, whom I proudly claim as one of my teachers, once said rather casually, 'The key to man's destiny is his ability to reinterpret what he cannot deny.' This simple observation is one of the most profoundly optimistic statements about human nature I know. . . . This book, to my mind, is in the tradition of Kelly's teachings, although it does not employ his particular vocabulary or techniques. (Bugental, 1976: 283n2)

Ray Holland called Kelly 'a reluctant existentialist' (1970). He saw Kelly's denial that he was an existentialist as an attempt to emphasize differences between personal construct theory and other theories. However, Joshua Soffer takes issue with Holland and says the differences Kelly *thought* were there, between existentialism and personal construct theory, *are* there. In particular, Soffer focuses on Kelly's 'advancement of a radically ordered cosmology'. To be able to predict and anticipate change, you have to conceive of a universe 'whose unfolding is so exquisitely ordered that humans may gradually come to capture its replicative themes through their system of anticipations'. Soffer goes further to say:

> Such an outlook, I believe, merits recognition as a postexistential theory or, as Kelly (1963, p. 183) indicated 'a calculated step beyond the experiential psychologies of inner "inner" feelings'. (Soffer, 1990: 359)

Soffer cites Rogerian therapy (Rogers, 1959) as an example of existential approaches and notes that Kelly argued that there were substantial differences between the client-centred and the personal construct approaches. Looking for influences, we can see that the client-centred approach changed in the important respect of the therapist becoming actively involved in helping the client reconstrue. Soffer points out that Rogers actually borrowed the term 'personal construct' and defined it as 'an organization of hypotheses for meeting life' (Rogers, 1951: 191). Rogers later says: 'Personal constructs are tentatively reformulated to be validated against further experience' (Rogers, 1961: 153).

There is no doubt that personal construct psychotherapy is a 'humanistic' therapy in that it is very different from psychoanalytic or behavioural therapies. For instance, clients are not pushed or pulled by 'drives' or unseen 'psychic energy'. The person 'chooses' to move in the direction of greater extension or definition of their construing system which, in turn, enables them to make ever more valid predictions – leading to ever greater control over their personal world.

But Kelly was not concerned exclusively with the client's experience. He placed as much emphasis on behaviour – it is, after all, our way of testing out our construing. In addition, he was interested in the assessment and measurement of a client's construing. In this respect he comes under Joseph Rychlak's heading of 'rigorous humanism' (1977). This is Kelly's clear influence on humanism. He showed how the experiential, the behavioural and measurement could be combined within one approach.

Once again we have an example of Kelly's influence as a teacher. This time it is supplied by Joseph Rychlak, who talks about the act of writing his book *A Philosophy of Science for Personality Theory* and how lonely it felt to start with. He goes on to say:

> But before long you must admit the truth and seek a certain sympathy if not support from others. You then realize that, even in the beginning, you had turned to others using the inspiration of an admired professor through your old class notes. Looking back, I can now thank Julian B. Rotter for teaching me how to think in research design terms, and George A. Kelly for showing me that data need not dictate the terms at every turn. (Rychlak, 1968: x)

Kelly's Influence on the Practice of Psychotherapy

The Introduction of a Practical Eclecticism

Kelly provided an anchor for his abstract theory by linking it to practicalities, such as assessment and measurement. This frees the personal construct psychotherapist from being tied to any particular *method* for helping the client reconstrue. The choice of method is determined by the 'transitive diagnosis' which, in turn, has been created under the guidance of the very complex and explicit theory.

It is easy to underestimate the importance of the freedom of action Kelly suggested the psychotherapist might have. But personal construct theory is not for the therapist who likes the security of having a defined set of procedures for any specific problem facing the client. Freedom in any context places additional responsibility on that person to choose well, and solely in the interests of the client. Therapeutic freedom can easily become a chance for the therapist to satisfy his or her own curiosity rather than being solely related to the needs of the client.

Psychotherapy with Children

The influence here is not very clear. But personal construct work with children has shown steady growth since 1955. The major influence of Kelly's theory, without doubt, is his refusal to see development in terms of stages.

The implication for psychotherapy with children is that the therapist is not constrained in any way by the idea that a particular child has not reached a particular stage in his or her development. There are no prescribed ways of construing a child's thinking or behaving that need to be taken into account. There is only the world of the child as it is experienced by that child. The goal in therapy with a child is no different from the goal with an adult – to help that person get on the move again.

Some specific ways that have been developed for working with children are covered later in this chapter.

The Psychotherapeutic Relationship

Mahoney puts the relationship expounded by Kelly more than forty years ago within the modern constructivist framework, saying:

> The therapist is more than a consultant, confessor, or psychotechnician; he or she is a specially trained collaborator who recognizes that the ultimate power and responsibility for change lie with the client. Together, client and counselor develop a special form of intimacy and a very personal working relationship . . .
>
> As rendered here, then, constructivist psychotherapy is a very intimate and personalized exchange between human beings. . . . A bond of caring and trust is developed, and the therapeutic relationship becomes an interpersonal context in and from which the client is encouraged to examine, explore, and experiment with personal constructions. . . . This highly personal inquiry entails excursions to and from the edges of their current phenomenal universe, and the expansion of those boundaries is inherently an 'edging process'. (Mahoney, 1988: 307–8)

All that could have been written by George Kelly; which perhaps is not surprising, since he was among the first if not *the* first to bring the implications of his philosophy of constructive alternativism into the psychotherapeutic arena.

One point needs stressing here since it has been misinterpreted on occasion. Having 'a very intimate and personalized exchange' does not mean a personal construct psychotherapist necessarily discloses personal thoughts and feelings to the client. The therapist may well do so, but always with the aim of giving the client material he or she may be able to use as they move along 'the edges of their current phenomenal universe', as Mahoney says. For Kelly, the therapist's essential usefulness to the client is acting as validator of the client's construing.

The Development of Methods and Practices

The Elicitation of Constructs

McFall's Mystical Monitor did not start out as a procedure for eliciting personal constructs. It was developed from the personal construct theory idea that psychologists should conduct experiments *with* people rather than *on* people.

> Supposing we were to accept that, however formal and systematic the psychological experiment, it ought to be more akin to the kinds of experiments which novelists undertake with their readers, or children undertake with their parents, or lovers undertake with each other, than the kind of experiments which were undertaken by the stereotypical Victorian physicist who seems to be our current ideal. (Bannister and Fransella, 1986: 162)

McFall developed a way of experimenting that became known as 'McFall's Mystical Monitor'. The procedure is made available to the client but the client does not share the results with the therapist. The client talks into a tape-recorder, alone, with a clear understanding and agreement that they will erase the tape immediately they have finished recording and listened to the recording as much as they want. The suggestion is that, after about twenty minutes of saying whatever comes into one's head, the tape is rewound and played back. After that, one talks for another twenty minutes or so, play back and listen again. This process might be repeated three times.

The reason for the first talk and play-back is that people often say they are embarrassed during the first period and they feel they are talking *as if to an audience*. They are conscious of omitting things, making points, making excuses and all the things one does with an audience. However, after the first session, there comes the realization that they are only fooling themselves.

In McFall's work there were not really any 'results' such as you would expect from the usual psychological experiment. But when asked what was learned from the experiment, all those who took part said they had learned something important from it. The major difficulty experienced was the erasing of the tape afterwards. There was a feeling that they might be destroying something really important of which they were currently unaware.

This procedure can prove useful for those clients who have little confidence in talking to the therapist about major issues. There is some similarity between this and the psychoanalytic method of free association. But in the case of the Mystical Monitor, the person is totally free to conduct this experiment in any way he or she chooses as no one is ever going to hear what has been said. There will be no interpretations from a second party. All interpretations come from the person concerned.

In some ways a computer can serve this same purpose. You write into your computer whatever you like. You read it back and then delete it! But it seems probable that hearing one's own voice saying these things is important. Computer elicitation of constructs has been developed by a number of people. These interactive computer programmes aim to develop the 'learning conversation' and 'self-organized learning' (see, for example, Thomas and Harri-Augstein, 1985). Mildred Shaw uses the scientist model in her book *On Becoming a Personal Scientist*:

> Each personal scientist uses himself as participative subject matter, and construes and interprets the results in a personally meaningful way. To do this effectively a conversational method must be used. Psychology offers a variety of these from the interview to introspection, but within personal construct theory the technique of the repertory grid exhibits a 'scientific' tool with which to structure a conversation. The repertory grid has since come to be known as 'a hard tool for soft psychologists', and indeed, to date, is one of the best attempts to examine and bring into awareness the conceptual system built and held by an individual. (Shaw, 1980: 9)

These programmes enable the client to 'talk to the computer' using the repertory grid as the basic structure. The computer elicits constructs from the person, it analyses the information and then feeds the results back to that person. This goes further than playing back McFall's tape because the computer gives information about the *implications* of what the person has said. That is, the person is told about the *relationships* between their constructs and the elements. The client, for instance, could be told which people in their grid seem well defined, which seem to create problems and so forth. It is possible to decide to quit the programme, to define in greater detail the reasons why a certain person is a problem area, or to extend the enquiry into some new aspects of life.

These 'learning conversations' with the computer have mainly been used in contexts other than therapy. 'Therapy by computer' is not something that is likely to appeal greatly to many psychotherapists. However, those who have a computer available might like to experiment. For instance, if you have a client who is a chemist, who finds it difficult to be 'psychological' and talk freely, he might be glad to 'talk' to a familiar computer in the first instance. It is worth constantly bearing in mind that a personal construct therapist uses, as far as possible, the language of the client.

Don Bannister says of the work of Thomas and Harri-Augstein that they

> ride rough shod, on their way to larger goals . . . [over] the distinctions between teaching, training and therapy. These are now old and entrenched distinctions to which we have attached different psychologies, different professions and different languages. [They] argue that when we teach a child to read, or train someone to operate a capstan lathe, or work as a psychotherapist with the psychologically distressed, we are (or ought to be) enabling them to become self-organised learners and that self-organised learning is both the pathway to particular 'skills' and is also that very self-mastery which lies at the heart of creative change. (Bannister, 1985)

Laddering is a skill or 'art form' described by Denny Hinkle (1965). It requires sensitive ears attuned to hearing what the person is saying behind the words. Hinkle developed the method to test out one of his hypotheses stemming from Kelly's Organization Corollary ('Each person characteristically evolves, for their convenience in anticipating events, a construction system embracing ordinal relationships between constructs'). Hinkle's hypothesis was that the more 'superordinate' a construct is (the more abstract, the higher up the hierarchy of constructs), the more it will resist change.

The method involves the therapist in credulous listening, suspending their own personal construing and the subsuming of the client's construing. Often in the laddering process you are asking the person to consider aspects of their way of understanding the world which they have never thought of before. It is here that you need to be especially alert so as to hear when the person is beginning to feel uneasy about the route the explorations are taking. The illumination that often comes with laddering can be alarming and threatening as well as exciting and interesting.

Laddering consists of no more and no less than asking the question 'why?' The person is first asked which pole of a given construct he or she would prefer to describe them. For instance, the construct might be between being *someone who could just 'be'* and being *someone who wears a mask*. The client, in this instance, said he would prefer to be *someone who could just 'be'*. Now the 'why?' question. 'Why would you rather be someone who can just *be* as opposed to someone who *wears a mask*?' The question can be phrased in many ways. By repeatedly being asked 'why?' the person climbs the 'ladder' of their construing system. Alternative forms of question include 'What are the advantages, for you, of being someone who . . .?' Or 'Why is it important for you to be . . .

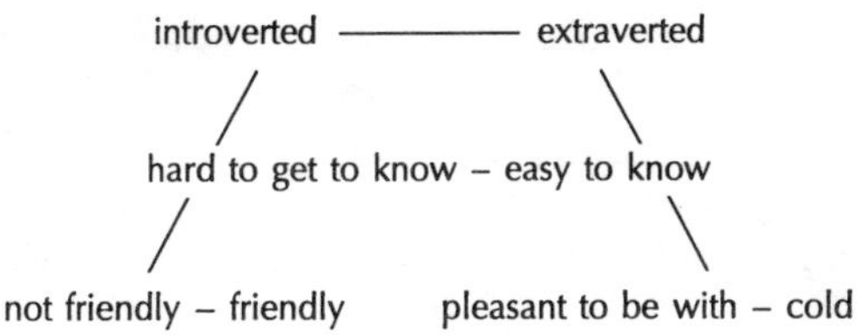

Figure 3 *Pyramiding*

rather than . . .?' There are no hard and fast rules. It is very much a skill which most people only acquire after considerable practice.

Ladders typically take you into the areas of the most superordinate constructs. These are constructs to do with what life is all about; life and death issues; religious constructs; what someone feels they cannot do without. You get straight into a person's basic system of values. It can be a far from peaceful business. Hinkle proved his point by showing that superordinate (laddered) constructs are, indeed, those that are most resistant to change.

Pyramiding This was described by Landfield in 1971 and is again related to the Organization Corollary and the hierarchy of constructs. It involves asking the person to successively 'climb down' their construct system to more and more concrete or subordinate levels. The questioning asks for more specific details of the construct. For example, 'What kind of a person is someone who is introverted?' The answer may be *hard to get to know*, as opposed to *easy to know*. The next question might be 'What kind of person is someone who is hard to get to know?' The same type of questioning then takes place with the opposite pole of the construct. In schematic form it looks like Figure 3.

To get to specific behaviours you can ask 'How do you know when a person is *cold*? What do they actually do that makes you think they are *cold*?' One such answer might be 'They look at you without blinking.'

This procedure can be particularly useful when you have a client who has specific inter-personal problems. You may want to do what in behaviour therapy terminology would be 'social skills training'. For instance, having found out what the personal meaning of being *cold* is for that person, you could use role playing to help the client look at various ways in which she, and others, might cope with a *cold* person. If the problem is that it is others who think *she* is cold, then the same procedure can usefully be used to specify what, in her behaviour, others are construing as *cold*.

Landfield gives examples of how this procedure can be used specifically to help the client reconstrue.

> In one instance it was used with a woman who feared dogs, but whose greatest dog was her husband that she had praised to the skies. The use of the procedure led to a pairing of dog with husband. Her husband had beaten her. (Landfield, personal communication)

Implicative dilemmas and the 'ABC' method Hinkle (1965) talked about 'implicative dilemmas' when referring to an ambiguous relationship between two constructs. The example he gave was between the constructs *realism vs idealism* and *desirable vs undesirable*. The person said that both *realism* and *idealism* had *desirable* and *undesirable* aspects for him. It was found that this person was using one construct label for two independent constructs – *testing ideas vs not testing ideas* and *not having goals vs having goals*. Hinkle points out that ambiguity in the implications between constructs means that the person cannot use those constructs effectively.

Finn Tschudi (1977) elaborated Hinkle's notion of 'implicative dilemmas' into a procedure he calls the ABC-model. In 1984, Finn Tschudi and Sigrid Sandsberg published an analysis they had carried out on a description of therapy with a client given by Don Bannister and me in *Inquiring Man* (Bannister and Fransella, 1971: 192). That client had a phobia of travelling and of telephones. He had a year of behaviour therapy which was successful. He was able to travel and to use the telephone without fear. However, far from being pleased, the client was totally dejected. He saw the whole exercise as pointless. He had nowhere to travel to and no one to ring up. He then had about two years of psychotherapy focusing on helping him establish his relationships with his peers. After this he was able to go anywhere he wanted and to visit his newly found friends, involving mainly superficial chit-chat with men, and joining various hobby groups. But he now pointed out that this was useless to him since what he really needed was a deep, passionate and intense sexual relationship with a woman.

Tschudi and Sandsberg's ABC-model of the client's construing can be seen in Figure 4.

This way of eliciting constructs can be highly informative for therapist and client alike. However, like all potentially powerful methods, it needs to be used with care and at the right time. It would at best be meaningless and at worst highly damaging to ask someone who had stuttered all his life for the advantages of stuttering and the disadvantages of being fluent in the first few sessions of therapy. The fact that in time you and he may well come to see that stuttering has some advantages is irrelevant. If

A: the problem

a1 actual state	a2 desired state
can't use telephone or travel	*can telephone and travel*

The client is now asked the disadvantages of a1 and the advantages of a2.

B: for change

b1 disadvantages of a1	b2 advantages of a2
prevents social possibilities	*open to new social possibilities*

The next questioning elicits what it is that prevents movement.The client is asked for the advantages of the present state (a1) and the disadvantages of the desired state (a2).

C: what prevents movement

c1 advantages of a1	c2 disadvantages of a2
hides lack of friends	*will reveal lack of friends*

The problem is now redefined as a lack of friends; the advantage of not being able to use the telephone or travel is that this will *hide the lack of true love.* After that the problem became redefined again as being *lack of true love,* and the desired state as being to *obtain true love.*

Figure 4 *Tschudi and Sandsberg's ABC-model*

you hypothesize that the client will be unable to accept such a suggestion, then that is what counts.

There are also potential dangers in the use of all these methods. The danger lies in what they may lead a person to understand about their own construing. A person may be happily seeing themselves as someone who *takes things as they come.* As they explore their system by, say, laddering, they may start to see that the path along which they are moving is going to end up with some notion that people who *take things as they come* are those who *have no commitment in life.* For this person, having commitment to life is extremely important. You may have inadvertently moved straight into a vastly important implicative dilemma of which the person has become consciously aware for the first time. The psychotherapist may well see this as an important area to explore with the client, but only when the client is able to make use of and build upon the experience.

These methods for eliciting constructs often provide sufficient information in themselves for the initial transitive diagnosis of the problem to be made. However, it is sometimes necessary to get more information about the client's construing of the world by 'going beyond the words'. In that case, some form of repertory grid may be found useful.

Methods of Assessment

Repertory Grids It is no exaggeration to say that there has been an explosion in the field of what is now referred to as 'repertory grid technique' since 1955. Don Bannister was the first person to use a modified form of Kelly's Rep Test (using the ranking of the 'elements') in order to study the process of thought disorder found in some of those labelled as schizophrenic. He later used the grid to study this process in the context of therapy (discussed later in this chapter under 'applications to specific problems').

Bernard Adams and I (Fransella and Adams, 1966) were the first to report using a series of ranking grids with a client in a clinical context. The client was being treated for depression while serving a prison sentence for arson. The aim was to monitor changes in his construing during his psychological therapy with the psychiatrist, with a view to being able to prevent him from committing further acts of arson. A personal aim of mine was to try out this new tool for measuring what a person thinks and feels about aspects of their life.

It was a successful experiment from my point of view. The series of grids did show very meaningful change over time as well as indicating just how statistically reliable grid measures can be. From the psychiatrist's point of view, the results were not as he had hoped. His view was that people commit arson because of the sexual arousal that results from lighting fires. At the start of the grid series, the arsonist 'said' in grid terms that he did not know what sexual arousal had to do with setting fire to things. As his therapy with the psychiatrist progressed, he obviously thought about this in some depth and came to the conclusion he was definitely *not* the sort of person who gets sexual pleasure from lighting fires nor was he 'an arsonist'. In his terms he was doing something quite different – he was punishing wrong-doers; fire-lighting was more an act of ritual cleansing.

That was the first of many examples showing that people with well-established behaviours do not see themselves as society sees them. That is, an obese person does not see himself or herself as 'an obese person' (Fransella and Crisp, 1970); an alcoholic is not 'an alcoholic' (Hoy, 1973); a stutterer is not 'a stutterer' (Fransella, 1972); a drug addict is not 'a drug addict' (Stojnov, 1990). The behaviour has become a way of life. It is as if we all acknowledge that we are being treated for being obese, for being alcoholic and so forth, but we divorce ourselves from the stereotype of such people – 'I may drink too much and be being treated for alcoholism, but I am not like the group called "alcoholics" – I am me.'

As well as creating the 'laddering' procedure and the idea of implicative dilemmas, Denny Hinkle also created the implications and the resistance-to-change grids. The *implications grid* was designed to test his theory that the meaning of a personal construct lies in the implications it has and those which it implies. As already said, Hinkle showed how the more implications a construct has, the more superordinate it is, and the more it will resist change. He created a *resistance-to-change* grid to test the latter. All these aims were realized. Since then, the research work of several people has supported Hinkle's findings that the more important (superordinate, laddered) constructs are to people, the more likely they are to resist change (for example, Fransella, 1972; Button, 1980).

When I started my inquiry about stuttering in the mid-1960s I found that Hinkle's implications grid method was too complicated to use with most people who were not university students, as they were in Hinkle's sample. I therefore simplified it so that the implications of each pole of each construct were explored. It was from this that I found evidence for the idea that the pole of the constructs on which we decide to place ourselves is the one that has the most meaning for us. That is, most psychotherapists will have more implications to do with *being caring* than *being uncaring*. Evidence that our client places themself on the less meaningful pole of any of their important constructs can help in our transitive diagnosis.

Over the years grid technology has sometimes become divorced from its personal construct theory roots. Where this happens, a problem arises because every measuring instrument has underlying assumptions that have to be adhered to. When divorced from their origins, these assumptions get forgotten.

A detailed account of these and other basic forms of grid can be found in *A Manual for Repertory Grid Technique* (Fransella and Bannister, 1977).

Self-Characterizations The other method of assessment Kelly devised was the self-characterization. But it has not been anything like as widely used as the repertory grid. This is probably because it has no easy method of analysis. It is clear, however, that many personal construct therapists and counsellors use it routinely. It has been developed in a number of ways: for instance, as the main method for facilitating reconstruing in a person who takes naturally to writing (Fransella, 1980).

Sharon Jackson and Don Bannister (1985) developed the self-characterization for work with children who have and who do not have problems. They showed how it was possible to develop scores that can give a meaningful impression of how 'good a psychologist' the child is. For example, there is the '"view of others" score: a count of the number of times the child refers to the view taken of him or her by other people'. Jackson uses this in her group work with disturbed children.

Davis et al. (1989) have described the 'child characterization sketch' for use with parents. This is a flexible method for eliciting and exploring in depth how mothers construe their children. The authors' specific concern was to understand how parents construe their intellectually impaired children (Cunningham and Davis, 1985). But it can just as easily be used with parents of children without physical, intellectual or emotional difficulties.

The Development of Group Work

Landfield and Rivers (1975) talked about ways of improving social relationships by using 'rotating dyads' in groups. These are now called *Interpersonal Transaction (IT) Groups*. Originally, at the beginning and end of each group session each participant wrote down how they felt at that time. They then pinned this 'mood tag' on themselves and walked about the room. In between, members spent a great deal of time in pairs. The pairs would only have about five to six minutes with each other and everyone would have the opportunity to interact with everyone else in the group. All were given a topic or area they were to discuss when in pairs, with the general aim that they should try to understand each other without being critical. After the second 'mood tag' all would come together for a group discussion lasting for at least fifteen minutes.

As Neimeyer (1988) points out, one important aspect of the IT group is that it describes the form of the group but not its content. This means it can be adapted for many purposes. Neimeyer lists eight other advantages of the IT format:

1 It promotes more rapid *self-disclosure*.
2 It encourages the development of *empathy*.
3 It facilitates higher levels of *group cohesion*.
4 It *evens out group participation* because everyone has to contribute equally.
5 There is less likelihood of there being conflict because the material for group discussion is provided by all.

6 It *focuses interactions* on relevant topics and thus makes maximum use of the time available.
7 It can be used for both open groups (where membership varies) and closed groups (where membership is the same throughout).
8 Members experience both the supportive, listening role and the client role.

Neimeyer concludes by saying that the key to the 'intelligent' use of the IT structure is its flexibility. He also provides some useful discussion topics for the dyads and questions that may be asked to promote discussion in the whole group.

Neimeyer and his colleagues have used IT groups with those having many problems including depression, alcohol abuse and post-traumatic stress disorder. But in particular they have used IT groups in the context of child abuse (Harter and Neimeyer, 1995). For an account of fifteen years' research on IT groups see Neimeyer et al. (1995).

The Application of Personal Construct Theory to Specific Psychological Problems

One of the major developments over the past fifty years has been the application of Kelly's theory to specific psychological problems. Personal construct theory has been described as a skeleton without any flesh. These authors have been attempting to put some flesh on that skeleton. So much research work has been carried out that selection has been difficult. The criteria used for selecting the following has been i) that the work has been based on a theory of the problem that stems directly from personal construct theory, and/or ii) that a method has been developed that may be of use to other psychotherapists or counsellors.

These examples are not intended to be presented as 'the truth' about the disorders. Rather, they are given as examples of what people have been doing with George Kelly's ideas over the past forty years. Anyone wanting an academic assessment of them is referred to David Winter's book *Personal Construct Psychology in Clinical Practice* (1992).

Bannister and Schizophrenic Thought Process Disorder

Bannister used Kelly's suggestion that this problem be linked with the professional construct of 'loose' construing. The language of someone diagnosed as suffering from thought process disorder associated with schizophrenia is incomprehensible in its extreme form. Bannister used as an example the following question sent by such a person to a British Broadcasting Corporation Brains Trust:

> A Darwinian biologist in the Greco-Roman war escapes by studying Afro-Asian sociology in a Grecian way and social sciences in a Roman way; Wolfenden is the Chairman of the National Security Council. What is the future of the branch of this tree? I am an air force blue mouse. (Bannister and Fransella, 1986: 143)

Apart from being an unfair question and having certain poetic qualities, it is incomprehensible to most people. However, incomprehensibility is not, in itself, sufficient to place one in the diagnostic category of 'schizophrenia'. Otherwise many renowned atomic physicists, mathematicians or even philosophers would be included. We, as members of society, would usually agree that the language of these people is just incomprehensible to us, and that it is probably highly interesting to those who know the private language. It is our problem, not theirs.

In the case of the thought-disordered schizophrenic person, the language is so private that probably no one else in the world could make sense of it. Also, the person is unable to use any other sort of language. Whereas the atomic physicist goes home and is most probably able to change to something approaching a social language that all can share, the thought-disordered person said to be suffering from schizophrenia would not be able to.

Using grids, Bannister (1962) showed that it was possible to 'measure' the degree of 'looseness' in the thinking of the thought-disordered schizophrenic which differentiated them from others who were not so afflicted. One of the contributions Bannister made to our understanding of this disorder was to show that these constructs are not loose to the point of destruction. Theoretically, we have subsystems of personal constructs. Personal construct theory is not a trait theory. Thus, a person may be very articulate and tight in their construing of machinery, but when it comes to construing people they can make little sense of them at all. So with the schizophrenic person. Bannister and Salmon (1966) showed that those with thought disorder are very much more organized (tighter) at construing objects than they are at construing people. Here was something that could be built on.

Using a constructive alternativist approach to scientific enquiry, Bannister found himself faced with the next question. If people who are thought-disordered do, indeed, have such loose constructions about the world of people that they cannot ever test out those constructions and make predictions, how did they get like that?

He then conducted a series of experiments to test the hypothesis that people become like that because of 'serial invalidation' (Bannister, 1965). Perhaps their expectations had been proved wrong over the years and, to deal with this, they had continually made their predictions less and less specific. He showed that this happened with so-called 'normal' people when they were asked to judge the characters of those in photographs and then were told they were not very good at it. He concluded that this

> suggests that thought-disordered people have been wrong too often. They are like scientists whose theories have been so often disproved that they have gone out of the theory-making business. (Bannister and Fransella, 1986: 147)

Another question was raised by this research. If this might be how people become thought-disordered, how can they be helped to tighten their construing once more so as to become thought-ordered? Therefore his next research programme was to find out what structure remained in their construing of people, again using grids. Having identified this residual structure, he set up situations that encouraged the schizophrenic person to 'see' people in those terms and thus provide them with some validation. He concluded that his results suggested that there was a way back for these clients, 'long and arduous though that journey may be' (Bannister et al., 1975).

A Personal Construct Approach to Those Who Stutter

Still in those early times of the 1960s, I started a piece of research into a personal construct theory treatment of stuttering. This work was finally published in 1972 and has influenced many speech therapists in how they approach helping those who stutter. There are now several books published on the subject (for example, Dalton, 1994).

I give an account of the work here in some detail in order to show how personal construct theory can be applied in a new context. My aim for the research was three-fold. I wanted to see whether this new theory, which I found so personally attractive, would be able to give me insights into something so clearly behavioural as a stutter. Could personal construct theory lead me to a therapy approach that would at least help those who stutter to approach fluency? Would it be possible to show a relationship between construing and a specific piece of behaviour?

I cannot say the process was easy. There was much pulling of hair and grinding and gnashing of teeth. But I found the way forward in the PhD dissertation just written by Dennis Hinkle (1965). This work had more exciting ideas in it than any I had read before or have read since. Some of them I have already mentioned, but two of his ideas were of prime importance for me. One stemmed from his basic thesis, that Kelly's notion of the personal construct can better be defined in terms of the 'implications' it has. You cannot know what *exciting* is unless you find out what it implies and what is implied by *being exciting*. Incidentally, Hinkle was the PhD student of George Kelly's who had the audacity to say, 'Professor Kelly, I do not know what a *construct* is.' So Hinkle set out to define it. But it was Hinkle's discussion of the Choice Corollary that I latched on to most firmly.

Hinkle's re-definition of the Choice Corollary runs thus:

> A person chooses for themselves that alternative in a dichotomized construct through which he anticipates the greater possibility for increasing the total number of implications of his system. That is to say, a person always chooses in that direction which he anticipates will increase the total meaning and significance of his life. Stated in the defensive form a person chooses so as to avoid the anxiety of chaos and the despair of absolute certainty. (Hinkle, 1965: 21)

My argument started to go like this. People *choose* for themselves that pole of a construct that is most meaningful to them. If that be so, then people continue to stutter because that is a more meaningful way of behaving than being fluent. 'Being more meaningful' in personal construct theory terms means the person is better able to predict or anticipate events. If that be the case, then any therapy for those who stutter should focus on fluent and not disfluent speech. My therapy now had its focus of attention. Being fluent needed to be made more meaningful than stuttering. This approach did not, of course, make everyone fluent overnight, nor over a long time in some cases. But there was clear evidence that many were greatly helped.

Having a personal interest in measurement, I used the 'implications grid' that Hinkle described. However, I used my own modification of the 'bi-polar implications grid' that looks at each pole of a construct separately. This started my continuing interest in the meanings of the opposite poles of constructs. In therapy I do think that, if you can really understand what a person is *not* doing by doing what they *are* doing, you have gained enormous understanding of why they continue to do what they say they do not want to do.

The results from the bi-polar implications grids showed that, as a person decreased their disfluent speech, so the *meaning* of being *fluent* increased. What I did not predict was that for this same person, the *meaning* of being *someone who stutters* decreased. It thus demonstrated a relationship between behaviour and construing. This may be something we now all know, but in a world in which behavioural methods were dominant, this was not such common knowledge. The study showed me that personal construct theory and its methods can be usefully applied to help those with quite difficult personal problems. Lastly, there was evidence that some were indeed helped by the use of personal construct psychotherapy.

Anorexia Nervosa

Soon after this work with stutterers finished, I applied the same ideas to those with weight disorders. It worked well with the obese. People who are very overweight see this as being a much more meaningful way of relating to the world than being a 'normal' weight.

However, early work with anorexic young women did not follow this pattern clearly at all. But the approach was taken up by Eric Button (1980) and he has devoted around twenty years to increasing our understanding of this distressing problem (Button, 1993). He rightly emphasizes that any general statement does not mean that all those diagnosed as suffering from anorexia nervosa construe in the same way. For instance, his research suggests that many anorexic girls have an unusually limited system for construing people, but not all. He says: 'Although they show similarities in some of their behaviour and attitudes, their view of the world is highly personal and crucial to any attempt to extricate them from the preoccupation with food and size issues' (Button, 1993: 211).

Depression and Suicide

There has been a considerable emphasis on applying personal construct ideas and methods to those experiencing depression. A central figure here has been Dorothy Rowe. She has written extensively to combat the widespread belief (not only among the medical world) that depression is a physical complaint best treated by drugs (Rowe, 1978; 1982; 1983). As has already been said, drugs can be important when the client is immobilized by their depressed feelings. But drugs alone will not help them reconstrue as they become more active.

Rowe argues that a child creates a series of constructs to do with interactions with others. Part of this system is concerned with how we prevent too much interaction. This construing helps form the wall we build around ourselves, perhaps under the heading 'I keep myself to myself'; 'I need my personal space.' She says:

> Some people build low walls, or walls with special gaps, and they can reach others easily across these walls. But some of us build walls which are high and difficult to climb, and when we make these walls too high, quite impassible, then we start to suffer a torture which is even worse than that suffered by a solitary prisoner facing an indeterminate sentence. (Rowe, 1978: 30)

Bob Neimeyer has carried out extensive research on depression within a personal construct framework (see Neimeyer, 1984; 1985b) and has greatly increased our knowledge of those who are depressed. He has also worked with Franz Epting on the development of a 'death threat index' (Epting and Neimeyer, 1984). Along with Dorothy Rowe, these authors see that a person's construing of death 'is central to the construct system because it determines how the purpose of life is construed' (Rowe, 1984: 11).

Neimeyer (1994) has summarized the literature on the threat index and provided a manual and scoring details. This index has been used to pinpoint concerns about death in hospice clients and to examine how death is construed in suicidal clients and also among the elderly.

Kelly has an unusual way of looking at the act of suicide. Everything has to be seen from the perspective of how the individual gives meaning to the world: so with suicide. In personal construct theory all behaviour is an experiment designed to test out the predictions stemming from the personal construing that is up for test. This means that the act of suicide is also an experiment designed to seek validation for something – one's life.

It will be remembered that Kelly said that the wages of guilt is death. Guilt is the perceived dislodgement from one's core construing. Core construing is that which gives the essential meaning to one's life. Perceived dislodgement from it means a person has the choice of living with it and trying to deal with it by reconstruing themselves, or of going along with it and seeing the termination of their life as the better way of extending or defining their way of dealing with the world. For example, the person may feel that they have behaved in such a contrary way to 'who I really am' that to continue to live with that guilt would mean living as 'not me' – an impossible situation to contemplate. The alternative is to eliminate that person in the anticipation that others will come to remember them as they were.

Hughes and Neimeyer (1990) report a personal construct model they have developed and tested out on people in hospital being treated for depression. Their findings suggest that those at highest risk of making an attempt to commit suicide have a construing system that shows fragmentation and pre-emptive (all-or-none) thinking.

Stefan and Von (1985) discuss the personal construct approach to suicide and give a detailed account of the different types of suicide which Kelly (1961) suggested might be useful to consider in relation to helping that person for whom the act has not been final.

Stefan and Linder take this further and outline a personal construct therapeutic approach to help such people. They end with this statement: 'In the course of preparing this chapter, we come to a remarkable conclusion, that through the treatment of suicidal individuals within the framework of personal construct psychology, one is engaging not in a morbid study of death but in a vibrant study of life itself' (Stefan and Linder, 1985: 208).

PCP as an Alternative to Behavioural Treatment

David Winter has written extensively and carried out much research on personal construct psychotherapy as an alternative to behavioural treatment approaches. One such approach is social skills training, described by Trower, Casey and Dryden as incorporating the following steps: '1) identification of the skill deficit; (2) instruction about the function of the skill; (3) role play demonstration of the skill; (4) client rehearsal of the skill; (5) feedback to the client about his performance; (6) client practice of the skill in real-life situations' (Trower et al., 1988: 95). At no point is the personal meaning of that skill the focus of attention.

Winter explains that personal construct psychotherapy takes the personal meaning of the skill as the starting point. When the advantages of, say, *being assertive* are explored it may well be found that these are actually 'undesirable' in the client's terms. For instance, *being assertive* might mean that *people do not like you*. It is possible that alternatives to being assertive may be found that are acceptable. Winter (1988a) has put these ideas to the test and has demonstrated the effectiveness of personal construct psychotherapy with a client whose condition had deteriorated during behavioural social skills training. Winter has also developed personal construct psychotherapy alternatives to the traditional behavioural approach to psychosexual problems (1988b) and agoraphobia (1989).

Ways of Working with Children

PCP work with children has not been widely written about. Some has been mentioned earlier in this chapter when discussing the uses of the self-characterization.

Jackson's group work with disturbed children (1992) is an interesting extension of personal construct psychotherapy into a very disturbed context. Her work with such groups started in 1985 and formed part of a research project into distinguishing between the construing of disturbed children and that of those who were deemed not to be disturbed.

The group procedure involved trying to understand each child's construing by using self-characterizations which the children were invited to share with the others. Each child also completed specially designed repertory grids and did individual and group drawings. The basic aim of the groups was to encourage the children to elaborate their construing of themselves.

Working with such disturbed children within a hospital setting was quite a problem. As Jackson says:

> Being unable to construe the group meetings as classroom activities, the children tried the broad constructions of the playground. Hence, some of the larger experiments involved complaints such as:
>
> a. calling the cardiac arrest team by using the attractive red buttons left unsealed in the ward; . . .
> c. telephoning for the firemen by dialling the written code on every telephone in nearby vacant nurse stations. (Jackson, 1992: 166)

In spite of such challenging behaviour, the therapy group children did, indeed, increase their self-esteem and elaborated their self-construing more than the control group. Of particular interest is the finding that the parents reported that none of the therapy group of eight children had re-offended or been suspended from school a year after therapy (Jackson, personal communication).

Tom Ravenette has been working with children in an educational context for over twenty years. One of his earliest publications was *Dimensions of Reading Difficulties* (1968). He says that only when he wrote this, did he fully appreciate Kelly's suggestion about a child with reading difficulties: 'Find out if the child likes the teacher.'

He came to see that the child referred to an educational psychologist may well be invalidating some important constructions the teacher has about themselves. In this context, he finds it useful to distinguish between 'difficulties' – which may be related to matters having few implications for a sense of self – and 'problems' – which may have powerful, albeit perhaps unrecognized, implications for a teacher's core constructs (Ravenette, 1977).

This has led him to the view that the referring teacher is his first client as it is the teacher who asks for help. The child may indeed have difficulties or problems, but they are not those for which the teacher has asked the psychologist's help.

Because of necessary time constraints within this context – often one session only – he developed many interviewing techniques, usable over a wide age range, which encourage the possibility of reconstruing on the part of the client (Ravenette, 1992).

At the heart of his interviewing practice is an elaborative enquiry involving the search for *contrast, implications, relevance, importance* and *experiencing* of the client's own responses. With teachers, he uses purely verbal approaches, relying heavily on reporting back fully what has transpired with the child. He sees this as providing a gentle way of challenging the teacher's existing constructions and opening the door to exploring the ways in which the child has perhaps invalidated the teacher's sense of self.

With children, he explores their ways of making sense of themselves and their circumstances using verbal methods, drawings and projective stories. Verbal methods include structured questions such as 'Who are you?' together with the elaborative enquiry mentioned above.

Drawings may be asked for to represent some of the answers given to the question 'Who are you?' They form the basis of the 'self-description grid' (Ravenette, 1978). These are ranked according to how each child thinks important people in his life might see him. He may also be asked to rank himself with his problem if it is felt that the child can 'use' the experience. Interviews may close by inviting the child to produce a story to some visual stimulus, usually a picture, and having the interviewer then give back a different story. The aim here is to integrate what the child has already given during the interview into an alternative understanding which makes sense and at the same time a story with alternative outcomes.

The whole enterprise is concluded with a full and elaborative discussion both with the teacher and head teacher, following the saying, 'If you want the wall to hear, talk to the door.' In such a meeting, alternative understandings and their implications in terms of actions can be envisaged.

Further details of Ravenette's work can be found in his 1985, 1988 and 1993 articles.

An Overview of the Influence of George Kelly

One way of tackling this question is to ask, as a personal construct psychotherapist might do, 'What would the state of psychotherapy be like if there had been no George Kelly?' Unfortunately, this does not seem to work well. We all live in a social and cultural context. Few people send the world on a totally different tack. For instance, one can only assume that without George Kelly spelling out his *constructive alternativism*, constructivism would have arisen within the context of psychotherapy in any case. Thus, I am going to speculate about what his influence seems to me to have been.

The man himself was a most complex character. His desire for privacy has meant that we are denied the possibility of knowing the ingredients that made up this complexity. But this is surely the norm for those who are called, by some at least, a genius. Without this complexity he could not have provided the world with the most complex, the most human, the most far-reaching and futuristic, and the most widely applicable theory about human individuals that has yet been devised. If there had not been areas of his construing that we feel might be better sorted out, would he have been so interested in the problems of others? Indeed, there can be few who do not have personal areas of difficulty. The conclusion on George Kelly the man must still be 'find him if you can'.

What of the influence of his work? One of the most important influences must surely have been on the development of constructivism within the field of psychotherapy. For Kelly made psychotherapy the focus of convenience of his theory. He gave the application of personal construct theory to psychotherapy as his example of its potential usefulness. Kelly was, in the terms of Joseph Rychlak (1981: 745) '. . . clearly and totally a Kantian-constructivist'. And 'he was purely a psychological constructivist'. This is a point that can easily get missed. Kelly, originally a physiological psychologist, excluded all organic constructions from his theory. He wanted such constructions left to those who owned them, such as the physiologists, the neurologists and the biologists. Nevertheless, he was not averse to speculating where a 'biological postulate' might get us.

But his emphasis on our processes 'being psychologically channelized . . .' frees us all from being trapped by the physical context within which we live – our body. Depression may, indeed, be related to some biochemical changes. But who is to say which is cause and which effect? If biochemical imbalance is seen as the cause of depression, then obviously drugs are necessary to correct that, and the person as a construing entity takes second place; the same with schizophrenia, stuttering or obesity. Diagnosis of brain damage most often implies that nothing can be done for that person. Personal construct theory says that is nonsense. That brain-damaged person is doing their best to make sense of the world *as they construe it*. Kelly gives us all permission to focus solely on the person as a construing entity and to try to help that person take control of their life again *within their physical and social context*. Contrary to what some say, the personal construct psychotherapist might even try to help the client improve their physical and social worlds wherever possible. The psychotherapist has to use their own limited abilities to get a glimpse of the client's world and help that client increase their control over it.

No doubt the cognitive therapies would have evolved at some stage, but Kelly certainly gave them a push. This was clearly not his intention, as the many varieties are still very much in the behavioural mode.

This highlights another of his influences on the work of the psychotherapist. Kelly was against the behavioural and the psychodynamic approaches for a variety of reasons. Not the least of these was the separation of the client from the therapist. He emphasized that the therapist is a person too who has no God-given rules about what is wrong with the client and how that client *should* become. The notion of reflexivity is deeply embedded in his theory. The psychotherapist has to be as much aware of their own construing as they are of the client's. In this sense, therapist and client are locked into a partnership in which the same theoretical rules apply. The same anxieties, the same threats, the same guilts may occur in each. The therapist is constantly on the look-out for any evidence of, say, hostility in themselves as much as in their client.

A final point is that Kelly gave us a philosophy and psychology that applies to all of life and is not limited to psychotherapy. He just chose psychotherapy as the focal point of his theory as he saw this as the best way to indicate its fertility.

His view of psychotherapy is summed up in the following:

> There is no particular kind of psychotherapeutic relationship – no particular kind of feelings – no particular kind of interaction that is in itself a psychotherapeutic panacea, nor is there any particular set of techniques that are the techniques of choice for the personal construct theorist. The relationships between therapist and client and techniques they employ may be as varied as the whole human repertory of relationships and techniques. It is the orchestration of techniques and the utilization of relationships in the on-going process of living and predicting from experience that makes psychotherapy a contribution to human life. (Kelly, 1969k: 223)

Select Bibliography of Kelly's Works

Kelly, G. A. (1959) *The Function of Interpretation in Psychotherapy: I. Interpretation as a way of life; II. Reinterpretation and personal growth; III. Techniques of psychotherapeutic reinterpretation*. London: Centre for Personal Construct Psychology; in conjunction with Wollongong: Personal Construct Group.

Kelly, G. A. (1970) 'A brief introduction to personal construct theory'. In D. Bannister (ed.), *Perspectives in Personal Construct Psychology*. London: Academic Press. Reprinted, 1985, London: Centre for Personal Construct Psychology.

Kelly, G. A. (1970) 'Behaviour is an experiment'. In D. Bannister (ed.), *Perspectives in Personal Construct Psychology*. London: Academic Press. Reprinted, 1985, London: Centre for Personal Construct Psychology.

Kelly, G. A. (1978) 'Confusion and the clock'. In F. Fransella (ed.), *Personal Construct Psychology 1977*. London: Academic Press.

Kelly, G. A. (1980) 'The psychology of optimal man'. In A. W. Landfield and L. M. Leitner (eds.), *Personal Construct Psychology: psychotherapy and personality*. New York: Wiley.

Kelly, G. A. (1991) *The Psychology of Personal Constructs*, (2 volumes). London: Routledge; in association with the Centre for Personal Construct Psychology. First published in 1955.

Maher, B. (ed.) (1969) *Clinical Psychology and Personality: selected papers of George Kelly*. New York: Wiley.

References

Adams-Webber, J. (1990) 'Personal construct theory and cognitive science', *International Journal of Personal Construct Psychology*, 3, 415–21.

Adler, A. (1937) 'Psychiatric aspects regarding individual and social disorganization', *American Journal of Sociology*, 42, 773–80.

Bannister, D. (1959) 'An Application of Personal Construct Theory (Kelly) to Schizoid Thinking'. Unpublished PhD thesis, University of London.

Bannister, D. (1962) 'The nature and measurement of schizophrenic thought disorder', *Journal of Mental Science*, 20, 104–20.

Bannister, D. (1965) 'The genesis of schizophrenic thought disorder: re-test of the serial invalidation hypothesis', *British Journal of Psychiatry*, 111, 377–82.

Bannister, D. (1966) 'Psychology as an exercise in paradox', *Bulletin of the British Psychological Society*, 19(63), 21–6.

Bannister, D. (1977) 'The logic of passion'. In D. Bannister (ed.), *New Perspectives in Personal Construct Theory*. London: Academic Press.

Bannister, D. (1981) 'The psychology of politics and the politics of psychology'. Unpublished talk given at the Centre for Personal Construct Psychology, London.

Bannister, D. (1985) 'Foreword'. In L. Thomas and S. Harri-Augstein, *Self-Organised Learning*. London: Routledge.

Bannister, D., Adams-Webber, J., Penn, W. I. and Radley, A. R. (1975) 'Reversing the process of thought disorder: a serial validation experiment', *British Journal of Social and Clinical Psychology*, 14, 169–80.

Bannister, D. and Fransella, F. (1966) 'A grid test of schizophrenic thought disorder', *British Journal of Social and Clinical Psychology*, 5, 95–102.

Bannister, D. and Fransella, F. (1971) *Inquiring Man*. Harmondsworth: Penguin Books.

Bannister, D. and Fransella, F. (1986) *Inquiring Man* (3rd edn). London: Routledge.

Bannister, D. and Mair, J. M. M. (1968) *The Evaluation of Personal Constructs*. London: Academic Press.

Bannister, D. and Salmon, P. (1966) 'Schizophrenic thought disorder: specific or diffuse?', *British Journal of Medical Psychology*, 39, 215–19.

Barry (1948) 'Kelly on role therapy and theory'. Unpublished raw data.

Bartlett, F. C. (1932) *Remembering: a study in experimental and social psychology*. Cambridge: Cambridge University Press.

Beck, A. T., Rush, A. J., Shaw, B. E. and Emery, G. (1979) *The Cognitive Therapy of Depression*. New York: Guilford.

Bohm, D. (1980) *Wholeness and the Implicate Order*. London: Routledge and Kegan Paul.

Bourland, D. D. and Johnston, P. D. (1991) *To Be or Not: an E-prime anthology*. San Francisco: International Society for General Semantics.

Brumfitt, S. (1985) 'The use of repertory grids with aphasic people'. In N. Beail (ed.), *Repertory Grid Technique and Personal Constructs: applications in clinical and educational settings*. Beckenham: Croom Helm.

Brumfitt, S. and Clarke, P. R. F. (1983) 'An application of psychotherapeutic techniques to the management of aphasia'. In C. Code and D. J. Müller (eds.), *Aphasia Therapy*. London: Edward Arnold.

Bruner, J. S. (1956) 'A cognitive theory of personality', *Contemporary Psychology*, 1, 355.

Bugental, J. (1976) *The Search for Existential Identity*. New York: Jossey-Bass.

Button, E. (1980) 'Construing and Clinical Outcome in Anorexia Nervosa'. Unpublished PhD thesis, University of London.

Button, E. (1993) *Eating Disorders: personal construct therapy and change*. Chichester: Wiley.

Cleanthous, C. C., Zelhart, P. F., Jackson, T. T. and Markley, R. P. (1982) 'George Kelly's "Rules": a code of conduct for psychologists, circa 1936', *University Forum*, 28, Fort Hays State University.

Conrad, J. (1906) *The Mirror of the Sea*. London: J. M. Dent and Sons Ltd.

Cooper, C. (1982) 'The group as an experiment'. Unpublished talk given at the Centre for Personal Construct Psychology, London.

Cummins, P. (1992) 'Reconstruing the experience of sexual abuse', *International Journal of Personal Construct Psychology*, 5, 355–65.

Cunningham, C. and Davis, H. (1985) *Working with Parents: frameworks for collaboration*. Milton Keynes: Open University Press.

Dalton, P. (1994) *Counselling People with Communication Problems*. London: Sage Publications.

Davis, H., Stroud, A. and Green, L. (1989) 'Child characterization sketch', *International Journal of Personal Construct Psychology*, 2, 322–37.

Dewey, J. (1933) *How We Think: a restatement of the relation of reflective thinking in the educative process* (2nd edn). Boston: Heath. First published, 1910.

Dewey, J. (1938) *Logic: the theory of inquiry*. New York: Holt, Rinehart and Winston.

Durkheim, E. (1933) *The Division of Labor in Society*. New York: Macmillan.

Durkheim, E. (1961) *Elementary Form of the Religious Life*. New York: Macmillan.

Einstein, A. and Infeld, I. (1938) *The Evolution of Physics*. Cambridge: Cambridge University Press.

Ellis, A. (1958) 'Rational psychotherapy', *Journal of General Psychology*, 59, 35–49.

Ellis, A. (1975) *How to Live with a Neurotic* (2nd edn). North Hollywood: Wilshire Book Co.

Ellis, A. (1976) *Sex and the Liberated Man* (2nd edn). Secaucus, NJ: Lyle Stuart.

Ellis, A. (1977) *Anger: how to live with and without it* (2nd edn). Secaucus, NJ: Citadel Press.

Epting, F. R. and Neimeyer, R. A. (eds.) (1984) *Personal Meanings of Death: applications of personal construct theory to clinical practice*. Baskerville: Hemisphere Publishing Company.

Frank, P. (1947) *Einstein: his life and times*. New York: Alfred A. Knopf.

Fransella, F. (1972) *Personal Change and Reconstruction: research on a treatment of stuttering*. London: Academic Press.

Fransella, F. (1980) 'Nature babbling to herself: the self characterisation as a therapeutic tool'. In J. G. J. Bonarius and S. Rosenberg (eds.), *Recent Advances in the Theory and Practice of Personal Construct Psychology*. London: Macmillan.

Fransella, F. (1983) 'What sort of person is the person as scientist?' In J. Adams-Webber and J. Mancuso (eds.), *Applications of Personal Construct Theory*. London: Academic Press.

Fransella, F. (1984) 'The relationship between Kelly's constructs and Durkheim's representations'. In R. Farr and S. Moscovici (eds.), *Social Representations*. Paris: Maison des sciences de l'Homme; Cambridge: Cambridge University Press.

Fransella, F. (1989) 'What is a construct?' In *Attributes, Beliefs and Constructs in Counselling Psychology* (occasional paper, Counselling Section BPS). Leicester: British Psychological Society, pp. 21–5.

Fransella, F. (1991) 'The construct of resistance in psychotherapy'. In G. Dunnett and L. Leitner (eds.), *Critical Issues in Personal Construct Psychotherapy*. New York: Krieger.

Fransella, F. and Adams, B. (1966) 'An illustration of the use of repertory grid technique in a clinical setting', *British Journal of Social and Clinical Psychology*, 5, 51–62.

Fransella, F. and Bannister, D. (1967) 'A validation of repertory grid technique as a measure', *Acta Psychologica*, 26, 97–106.

Fransella, F. and Bannister, D. (1977) *A Manual for Repertory Grid Technique*. London: Academic Press.

Fransella, F. and Crisp, A. H. (1970) 'Conceptual organisation and weight change', *Psychosomatics and Psychotherapy*, 18, 176–85.

Goffman, E. (1968) *Asylums*. London: Penguin.

Harré, R. (1982) *The Social Construction of Emotions*. Oxford: Blackwell.

Harré, R. and Lamb, R. (eds.) (1983) *The Encyclopedic Dictionary of Psychology*. Oxford: Blackwell.

Harter, S. L. and Neimeyer, R. A. (1995) 'Long term effects of child sexual abuse: toward a constructivist theory of trauma and its treatment'. In R. A. Neimeyer and G. J. Neimeyer (eds.), *Advances in Personal Construct Psychology* (Volume 3). Greenwich, CN: JAI.

Hinkle, D. N. (1965) 'The Change of Personal Constructs from the Viewpoint of a Theory of Construct Implications'. Unpublished PhD dissertation, Ohio State University.

Hinkle, D. N. (1970) 'The game of personal constructs'. In D. Bannister (ed.), *Perspectives in Personal Construct Theory*. London: Academic Press.

Holland, R. (1970) 'George Kelly: constructive innocent and reluctant existentialist'. In D. Bannister (ed.), *Perspectives in Personal Construct Theory*. London: Academic Press.

Holland, R. (1981) 'From perspectives to reflexivity'. In H. Bonarius, R. Holland and S. Rosenberg (eds.), *Personal Construct Psychology: recent advances in theory and practice*. London: Macmillan.

Hoy, R. M. (1973) 'The meaning of alcoholism for alcoholics: a repertory grid study', *British Journal of Social and Clinical Psychology*, 12, 98–9.

Hughes, S. L. and Neimeyer, R. A. (1990) 'A cognitive model of suicidal behavior'. In D. Lester (ed.), *Understanding Suicide: the state of the art*. New York: Charles Press.

Jackson, S. (1992) 'A PCT therapy group for adolescents'. In P. Maitland and D. Brennan (eds.), *Personal Construct Theory Deviancy and Social Work*. London: Inner London Probation Service and the Centre for Personal Construct Psychology.

Jackson, S. and Bannister, D. (1985) 'Growing into self'. In D. Bannister (ed.), *Issues and Approaches in Personal Construct Theory*. London: Academic Press.

Jackson, T. T., Zelhart, P. F., Markley, R. P. and Guydish, J. (1982) 'Kelly's polar adjectives: an anticipation of the semantic differential', *University Forum*, 28, Fort Hays State University.

Jahoda, M. (1988) 'The range of convenience of personal construct psychology: an outsider's view'. In F. Fransella and L. Thomas (eds.), *Experimenting with Personal Construct Psychology*. London: Routledge.

Jones, H. (1985) 'Creativity and depression: an idiographic study'. In F. Epting and A. W. Landfield (eds.), *Anticipating Personal Construct Psychology*. Nebraska: Nebraska University Press.

Kelly. G. A. (1927) 'A plan for socializing Friends University with respect to student participation in school control'. Unpublished manuscript, Kansas University. Copies at the Centre for Personal Construct Psychology, London and the University of Nebraska.

Kelly, G. A. (1930) 'The social inheritance'. In P. Stringer and D. Bannister (eds.), *Constructs of Sociality and Individuality*, 1979. London: Academic Press.

Kelly, G. A. (1932) 'Understandable psychology'. Unpublished manuscript. Copies at the Centre for Personal Construct Psychology, London and the University of Nebraska.

Kelly, G. A. (1936) 'Handbook of clinic practice'. Unpublished manuscript, Fort Hays State University.

Kelly, G. A. (1938) 'A method of diagnosing personality in the psychological clinic', *The Psychological Record*, 11, 95–111.

Kelly, G. A. (1953a) 'A preliminary inquiry leading to a plan for a comprehensive experimental study of the uses of television in teacher education'. Unpublished manuscript. Copies at the Centre for Personal Construct Psychology, London and the University of Nebraska.

Kelly, G. A. (1953b) *A Student's Outline of Graduate Training in Clinical Psychology in the Ohio State University*. Columbus, Ohio: Ohio State University.

Kelly, G. A. (1955a) *The Psychology of Personal Constructs* (2 volumes). New York: Norton. See Kelly (1991).

Kelly, G. A. (1955b) 'Television at the classroom door'. Unpublished manuscript. Copies at the Centre for Personal Construct Psychology, London and the University of Nebraska.

Kelly, G. A. (1958) 'Teacher–student relations at the university level'. Unpublished manuscript. Copies at the Centre for Personal Construct Psychology, London and the University of Nebraska.

Kelly, G. A. (1959a) 'Values, knowledge and social control'. Reprinted, 1989, London: Centre for Personal Construct Psychology; Wollongong: Personal Construct Group.

Kelly, G. A. (1959b) *The Function of Interpretation in Psychotherapy: 1. Interpretation as a way of life*. London: Centre for Personal Construct Psychology; Wollongong: Personal Construct Group.

Kelly, G. A. (1961) 'The personal construct point of view'. In N. Faberow and E. Shneidman (eds.), *The Cry for Help*. New York: McGraw-Hill.

Kelly, G. A. (1962) 'Muddles, myths and medicine', *Contemporary Psychology*, 7, 363–5.

Kelly, G. A. (1963) *The Theory of Personality: the psychology of personal constructs*. New York: Norton.

Kelly, G. A. (1965) Unpublished letter to Fay Fransella.

Kelly, G. A. (1966) Unpublished interview with Fay Fransella.

Kelly, G. A. (1969a) 'The autobiography of a theory'. In B. Maher (ed.), *Clinical Psychology and Personality: selected papers of George Kelly*. New York: Wiley.

Kelly, G. A. (1969b) 'Sin and psychotherapy'. In B. Maher (ed.), *Clinical Psychology and Personality: selected papers of George Kelly*. New York: Wiley.

Kelly, G. A. (1969c) 'The language of hypothesis: man's psychological instrument'. In B. Maher (ed.), *Clinical Psychology and Personality: selected papers of George Kelly*. New York: Wiley.

Kelly, G. A. (1969d) 'Personal construct theory and the psychotherapeutic interview'. In B. Maher (ed.), *Clinical Psychology and Personality: selected papers of George Kelly*. New York: Wiley.

Kelly, G. A. (1969e) 'Ontological acceleration'. In B. Maher (ed.), *Clinical Psychology and Personality: selected papers of George Kelly*. New York: Wiley.

Kelly, G. A. (1969f) 'The strategy for psychological research'. In B. Maher (ed.), *Clinical Psychology and Personality: selected papers of George Kelly*. New York: Wiley.

Kelly, G. A. (1969g) 'Humanistic methodology in psychological research'. In B. Maher (ed.), *Clinical Psychology and Personality: selected papers of George Kelly*. New York: Wiley.

Kelly, G. A. (1969h) 'Man's construction of his alternatives'. In B. Maher (ed.), *Clinical Psychology and Personality: selected papers of George Kelly*. New York: Wiley.

Kelly, G. A. (1969i) 'A mathematical approach to psychology'. In B. Maher (ed.), *Clinical Psychology and Personality: selected papers of George Kelly*. New York: Wiley.

Kelly, G. A. (1969j) 'Nonparametric factor analysis of personality'. In B. Maher (ed.), *Clinical Psychology and Personality: selected papers of George Kelly*. New York: Wiley.

Kelly, G. A. (1969k) 'The psychotherapeutic relationship'. In B. Maher (ed.), *Clinical Psychology and Personality: selected papers of George Kelly*. New York: Wiley.

Kelly, G. A. (1970a) 'A brief introduction to personal construct theory'. In D. Bannister (ed.), *Perspectives in Personal Construct Theory*. London: Academic Press. Reprinted, 1985, London: Centre for Personal Construct Psychology.

Kelly, G. A. (1970b) 'Behaviour is an experiment'. In D. Bannister (ed.), *Perspectives in Personal Construct Theory*. London: Academic Press. Reprinted, 1985, London: Centre for Personal Construct Psychology.

Kelly, G. A. (1973) 'Fixed role therapy'. In R. M. Jurjevich (ed.), *Direct Psychotherapy: 28 American originals*. Coral Gables: University of Miami Press. Manuscript also at Centre for Personal Construct Psychology, London.

Kelly, G. A. (1977) 'The psychology of the unknown'. In D. Bannister (ed.), *New Perspectives in Personal Construct Theory*. London: Academic Press.

Kelly, G. A. (1978) 'Confusion and the clock'. In F. Fransella (ed.), *Personal Construct Psychology 1977*. London: Academic Press.

Kelly, G. A. (1980) 'The psychology of optimal man'. In A. W. Landfield and L. M. Leitner (eds.), *Personal Construct Psychology: psychotherapy and personality*. Chichester: Wiley.

Kelly, G. A. (1991) *The Psychology of Personal Constructs* (2 volumes). London: Routledge. First published 1955.

Kelly, G. A. and Conrad, L. (1954) 'Report on classroom television'. Unpublished manuscript. Copies at the Centre for Personal Construct Psychology, London and the University of Nebraska.

Kelly, G. A. and Warnock, W. G. (1935) 'Inductive trigonometry'. Unpublished textbook, workbook, diagnostic tests and remedial exercises in trigonometry. Copy held at the University of Nebraska and part copy at the Centre for Personal Construct Psychology, London.

Korzybski, A. (1933) *Science and Sanity: an introduction to non-Aristotelian systems and general semantics*. Lakeville, CT: Institute of General Semantics.

Laing, R. D. (1967) *The Politics of Experience and the Bird of Paradise*. London: Penguin.

Landfield, A. W. (1971) *Personal Construct Systems in Psychotherapy*. Chicago: Rand McNally.

Landfield, A. W. and Rivers, P. C. (1975) 'An introduction to interpersonal transaction and rotating dyads', *Psychotherapy: Theory, Research and Practice*, 12, 366–74.

Lister-Ford, C. and Pokorny, M. (1994) 'Individual adult psychotherapy'. In P. Clarkson and M. Pokorny (eds.), *The Handbook of Psychotherapy*. London: Routledge.

Mackay, D. (1975) *Clinical Psychology: theory and therapy*. (Essential Psychology Series). London: Methuen.

MacKinnon, D. W. (1962) 'Nature and nurture of creative talent', *American Psychologist*, 17, 484–95.

Maher, B. (ed.) (1969) *Clinical Psychology and Personality: selected papers of George Kelly*. New York: Wiley.

Mahoney, M. J. (1988) 'Constructive metatheory: II. Implications for psychotherapy', *International Journal of Personal Construct Psychology*, 1, 299–315.

Mahoney, M. J. (1991) *Human Change Processes*. New York: Basic Books.

Mair, J. M. M. (1977) 'Metaphors for living'. In A. W. Landfield (ed.), *Nebraska Symposium on Motivation* (Vol. 24). Lincoln: University of Nebraska Press.

McWilliams, S. (1980) 'The choice corollary and preferred ways of being'. Unpublished manuscript.

McWilliams, S. A. (1988) 'On becoming a personal anarchist'. In F. Fransella and L. Thomas (eds.), *Experimenting with Personal Construct Psychology*. London: Routledge.

McWilliams, S. A. (1993) 'I accept, with pleasure, the invitation(al)'. Paper presented at the 10th International Congress on Personal Construct Psychology, Townsville, Australia.

Meichenbaum, D. H. (1977) *Cognitive Behavior Modification*. New York: Plenum.

Mischel, W. (1980) 'George Kelly's appreciation of psychology: a personal tribute'. In M. J. Mahoney (ed.), *Psychotherapy Process: current issues and future directions*. New York: Plenum Press.

Moreno, J. L. (1937) 'Inter-personal therapy and the psychopathology of inter-personal relations', *Sociometry: a Journal of Inter-Personal Relations*, 1, 9–76.

Moreno, J. L. (1964). *Psychodrama* (Vol. 1). Beacon, New York: Beacon House. First published 1946.

Moscovici, S. (1983) 'Social representation'. In R. Harré and R. Lamb (eds.), *The Encyclopedic Dictionary of Psychology*. Oxford: Blackwell.

Neimeyer, R. A. (1980) 'George Kelly as therapist: a review of his tapes'. In A. W. Landfield and L. M. Leitner (eds.), *Personal Construct Psychology: psychotherapy and personality*. New York: Wiley.

Neimeyer, R. A. (1984) 'Toward a personal construct conceptualization of depression and suicide'. In F. R. Epting and R. A. Neimeyer (eds.), *Personal Meanings of Death: applications of personal construct theory to clinical practice.* New York: Hemisphere/McGraw-Hill.

Neimeyer, R. A. (1985a) *The Development of Personal Construct Psychology.* Lincoln: University of Nebraska Press.

Neimeyer, R. A. (1985b) 'Personal constructs in depression: research and clinical implications'. In E. Button (ed.), *Personal Construct Theory and Mental Health.* London: Croom Helm.

Neimeyer, R. A. (1988) 'Clinical guidelines for conducting interpersonal transaction groups', *International Journal of Personal Construct Psychology*, 1, 181–90.

Neimeyer, R. A. (1994) 'The threat index and related methods'. In R. A. Neimeyer (ed.), *Death Anxiety Handbook: research, instrumentation and application.* New York: Taylor and Francis.

Neimeyer, R. A., Brooks, D. L. and Baker, K. D. (1995) 'Personal epistemologies and personal relationships: consensual validation and impression formation in the acquaintance process'. In B. Walker and D. Kelekin-Fishman (eds.), *The Construction of Group Realities.* Malabar, Florida: Krieger.

Neimeyer, R. A. and Mahoney, M. J. (eds.) (1995) *Constructivism in Psychotherapy.* Washington: American Psychological Association.

Novak, J. M. (1983) 'Personal construct theory and other perceptual pedagogies'. In J. Adams-Webber and J. C. Mancuso (eds.), *Applications of Personal Construct Theory.* Toronto: Academic Press.

Oliver, D. and Landfield, A. W. (1962) 'Reflexivity: an unfaced issue of psychology', *Journal of Individual Psychology*, 18, 114–24.

Osgood, C. E., Suci, G. J. and Tannenbaum, P. M. (1957) *The Measurement of Meaning.* Chicago: University of Illinois Press.

Peck, D. and Whitlow, D. (1975) *Approaches to Personality Theory* (Essential Psychology Series). London: Methuen.

Piaget, J. (1954) *The Construction of Reality in the Child.* New York: Basic Books. First published 1937.

Procter, H. and Parry, G. (1978) 'Constraint and freedom: the social origin of personal constructs'. In F. Fransella (ed.), *Personal Construct Psychology 1977.* London: Academic Press.

Raskin, J. and Epting, F. R. (1993) 'Personal construct theory and the argument against mental illness', *International Journal of Personal Construct Psychology*, 6, 351–69.

Ravenette, T. A. (1968) *Dimensions of Reading Difficulties.* Oxford: Pergamon Press.

Ravenette, T. A. (1977) 'Personal construct theory: an approach to the psychological investigation of children'. In D. Bannister (ed.), *New Perspectives in Personal Construct Theory.* London: Academic Press.

Ravenette, T. A. (1978) 'Children's self description grid: theme and variations' (abstract). In F. Fransella (ed.), *Personal Construct Psychology 1977.* London: Academic Press.

Ravenette, T. A. (1985) 'PCP and the professional who works with children'. Occasional paper, Centre for Personal Construct Psychology, London.

Ravenette, T. A. (1988) 'Personal construct psychology in the practice of an educational psychologist'. In G. Dunnett (ed.), *Working with People.* London: Routledge.

Ravenette, T. A. (1992) 'One-off case study'. In P. Maitland and D. Brennan (eds.), *Personal Construct Theory Deviancy and Social Work*. London: Inner London Probation Service/Centre for Personal Construct Psychology.

Ravenette, T. A. (1993) 'Transcending the obvious and illuminating the ordinary: PCP and consultation in the practice of an educational psychologist'. In L. Leitner and G. Dunnett (eds.), *Critical Issues in Personal Construct Psychotherapy*. Malabar, Florida: Krieger.

Rogers, C. R. (1951) *Client-Centred Therapy: its current practice, implications and theory*. Boston: Houghton Mifflin.

Rogers, C. R. (1956) 'Intellectualized psychotherapy', *Contemporary Psychology*, 1, 357–8.

Rogers, C. R. (1959) 'A theory of therapy, personality, and interpersonal relationships as developed in the client centered framework'. In S. Koch (ed.), *Psychology: a study of a science* (Vol. 3). New York: McGraw-Hill.

Rogers, C. R. (1961) *On Becoming a Person*. Boston: Houghton Mifflin.

Rosenhan, D. (1984) 'On being sane in insane places'. In P. Watzlawick (ed.), *Invented Reality: how do we know what we believe we know? Contributions to Constructivism*. New York: Norton.

Rowe, D. (1978) *The Experience of Depression*. Chichester: Wiley.

Rowe, D. (1982) *The Construction of Life and Death*. Chichester: Wiley.

Rowe, D. (1983) *Depression: the way out of the prison*. London: Routledge.

Rowe, D. (1984) 'Constructing life and death'. In F. R. Epting and R. A. Neimeyer (eds.), *Personal Meanings of Death: applications of personal construct theory to clinical practice*. Baskerville: Hemisphere Publishing Company.

Rychlak, J. F. (1968) *A Philosophy of Science for Personality Theory*. Boston: Houghton Mifflin.

Rychlak, J. F. (1977) *The Psychology of Rigorous Humanism*. New York: Wiley.

Rychlak, J. F. (1978) 'Dialectical features of Kellyian theorizing' (abstract). In F. Fransella (ed.), *Personal Construct Psychology 1977*. London: Academic Press.

Rychlak, J. F. (1981) *Introduction to Personality and Psychotherapy* (2nd edn). New York: Houghton Mifflin.

Shaw, M. L. (1980) *On Becoming a Personal Scientist*. London: Academic Press.

Simonton, O. K. and Creighton, J. (1978) *Getting Well Again*. New York: Bantam.

Soffer, J. (1990) 'George Kelly versus the existentialists: theoretical and therapeutic implications', *International Journal of Personal Construct Psychology*, 3, 357–76.

Stefan, C. and Linder, H. B. (1985) 'Suicide, an experience of chaos or fatalism: perspectives from personal construct theory'. In D. Bannister (ed.), *Issues and Approaches in Personal Construct Theory*. London: Academic Press.

Stefan, C. and Von, J. (1985) 'Suicide'. In E. Button (ed.), *Personal Construct Theory and Mental Health*. Beckenham: Croom Helm.

Stewart, A. E. and Barry, J. R. (1991) 'Origins of George Kelly's constructivism in the work of Korzybski and Moreno', *International Journal of Personal Construct Psychology*, 4, 121–36.

Stojnov, D. (1990) 'Construing HIV positivity amongst heroin addicts'. In P. Maitland and D. Brennan (eds.), *Personal Construct Theory Deviancy and Social Work*. London: Inner London Probation Service/Centre for Personal Construct Psychology.

Szasz, T. (1960) 'The myth of mental illness', *American Psychologist*, 15, 113–18.

Szasz, T. (1961) *The Myth of Mental Illness: foundations of a theory of personal conduct*. London: Hoeber.

Szasz, T. (1969) 'The crime of commitment', *Psychology Today*, 2, 55–7.

Szasz, T. (1970) *Idiology and Insanity: essays on the psychiatric dehumanization of man*. Garden City, New York: Doubleday Anchor.

Tajfel, H., Jaspars, M. F. J. and Fraser, C. (eds.) (1984) *The Social Dimension*. New York: Harper and Row.

Thomas, L. F. and Harri-Augstein, E. S. (1985) *Self-Organised Learning: foundations of a conversational science for psychology*. London: Routledge.

Trower, P., Casey, A. and Dryden, W. (1988) *Cognitive-Behavioural Counselling in Action*. London: Sage Publications.

Tschudi, F. (1977) 'Loaded and honest questions'. In D. Bannister (ed.), *New Perspectives in Personal Construct Theory*. London: Academic Press.

Tschudi, F. and Sandsberg, S. (1984) 'On the advantages of symptoms: exploring the client's construing', *Scandinavian Journal of Psychology*, 25, 69–77.

Vaihinger, H. (1924) *The Philosophy of 'As If': a system of the theoretical, practical and religious fictions of mankind* (translated by C. K. Ogden). London: Routledge and Kegan Paul.

Vasco, A. B. (1994) 'Correlates of constructivism among Portuguese therapists', *Journal of Constructivist Pyschology*, 7, 1–16.

Vaughan, C. M. and Pfenninger, D. T. (1994) 'Kelly and the concept of developmental stages', *Journal of Constructivist Psychology*, 7, 177–90.

Walker, B. M. (1992) 'Values and Kelly's theory: becoming a good scientist', *International Journal of Personal Construct Psychology*, 5, 259–69.

Warren, W. G. (1989) 'Personal construct theory and general trends in contemporary philosophy', *International Journal of Personal Construct Psychology*, 2, 287–300.

Warren, W. G. (1990) 'Is personal construct psychology a cognitive psychology?', *International Journal of Personal Construct Psychology*, 3, 393–414.

Warren, W. G. (1991) 'Rising up from down under: a response to Adams-Webber on cognitive psychology and personal construct theory', *International Journal of Personal Construct Psychology*, 4, 43–9.

Watson, J. B. (1913) 'Psychology as the behaviorist sees it', *Psychological Review*, 20, 158–77.

Watzlawick, P. (1984) 'Part 2: Effect or cause?' In P. Watzlawick (ed.), *Invented Reality: how do we know what we believe we know?* New York: Norton.

Webb, A. (1993) 'Cross-cultural issues', *Counselling News*, 9.

Winter, D. A. (1988a) 'Constructions in social skills training'. In F. Fransella and L. Thomas (eds.), *Experimenting with Personal Construct Psychology*. London: Routledge.

Winter, D. A. (1988b) 'Reconstructing an erection and elaborating ejaculation: personal construct theory perspectives on sex therapy', *International Journal of Personal Construct Psychology*, 1, 81–99.

Winter, D. A. (1989) 'An alternative construction of agoraphobia'. In K. Gournay (ed.), *Agoraphobia: current perspectives on theory and treatment*. London: Routledge.

Winter, D. A. (1992) *Personal Construct Psychology in Clinical Practice: theory, research and applications*. London: Routledge.

Index